African Customary Law

African Customary Law

Assessing Its Status and Effects Today

Casper Njuguna

LEXINGTON BOOKS
Lanham • Boulder • New York • London

Published by Lexington Books
An imprint of The Rowman & Littlefield Publishing Group, Inc.
4501 Forbes Boulevard, Suite 200, Lanham, Maryland 20706
www.rowman.com

6 Tinworth Street, London SE11 5AL, United Kingdom

British Library Cataloguing in Publication Information Available

Library of Congress Cataloging-in-Publication Data Available

ISBN: 978-1-4985-8440-1 (cloth)
ISBN: 978-1-4985-8441-8 (electronic)

I dedicate this book to my wife Glory Njuguna
and daughter Gabriella Njuguna.

Contents

Acknowledgments

Special acknowledgment to my parents, Bsh. Dr. and Rev. Armstrong and Rhoda Cheggeh, Ps. Elizabeth Njiru, and all siblings.

Special thanks and acknowledgment to Dr. Linda Camp Keith for all your advice and assistance in life and academia.

Chapter One

An Introduction to the Study of Customary Law

When studying Africa, whether the whole continent or a specific region, it is important to appreciate the sheer size and scope of the continent, and not relegate it to an examination that views Africa as a singular state. When examining a map, Africa appears to be roughly the size of the United States, leading most to examine it as if it were a nation-state. The actual size of Africa is the size of the United States, all Eastern Europe, India, China, Japan and the UK put together, without the inclusion of North Africa which would mean adding all Western Europe into the mix. It is noteworthy to see the students' faces who are amazed as they realize the sheer size of the continent that encompasses 54 sovereign UN recognized states with multiple ethnic formations and languages, and that share many share experiences whether legal or cultural. Therefore, anyone attempting to do African studies should approach the subject with as much vigor as caution for we have only tipped our understanding of African history, law and philosophy. For instance, while the earliest artistic expressions were argued to have been from 30,000 years ago with cave art found in France, recent discoveries have found cave art in South Africa demonstrating artistic expression on the continent dating back as far as 70,000 years (Louis Gates 2017). A unique part of sub-Saharan cultural and legal orientation that existed even prior to colonial occupation is that of customary law, which I term neo-autogenous sub-Saharan (NAS) law—"Neo" depicting its modified form mostly due to colonization and "autogenous" referring to the fact that it originally emerged from Africa independent of external influence. Sub-Saharan Africa is Africa south of the Sahara Desert. Neo-autogenous law continues to be part of the sub-Saharan experience. The conceptualization of customary law as NAS law is especially important for scholars and those who have no familiarity with sub-Saharan legal formations. Sub-Saharan states have modern legal colonial inherited systems coexisting alongside autogenous legal formations. Even while working on this book project, I have been party to several NAS law processes mostly around family law. Therefore, its continuous and high level of use requires an examination of its definitional framework. Table 1.1 describes some descriptive aspects of customary law that I discuss in greater detail in chapter 2.

Table 1.1. Descriptive Aspects of Customary Law

Aspect	*Characteristic*
Foundation	Based on stable original domestic principles
Time Limit	Continuous principles long time period
Dimension	Communal and cultural relativism
Parties	Practiced by distinct blood & marriage ethnic lineages
Jurisdiction	Property, marriage, rites of passage, gender, communal
Form	Usually not codified
Status	Coexist with other state law but not engrafted

In this chapter, I introduce some of the challenges and opportunities in the study of sub-Saharan customary law which provide much insight into customary law and the tensions surrounding it, especially, for a non-Africanist. Customary law continues to be one of the most important and quintessential forms of social organization and regulation in the sub-Saharan landscape. The topic is quite salient leading to a divide between proponents who defend its use and critics who argue for its removal. I have often found myself between the different perspectives on customary law, its use, and its future. Careful consideration should be given when examining the topic because of its salient nature which usually blurs the lines between personal views, empirical data and desired policy outcomes. The topics and issue areas include the experience a scholar or a student has with the study, including the view of customary law as a discrete legal type based on principles versus being mere customs, and the contradiction between global legal expectations and customary law. Despite the challenges, there are many opportunity areas that scholars can examine, including making a stronger definitional framework that conceptualizes customary law. Another opportunity area is the examination of how sub-Saharan states have legally dealt with customary law in their state constitutions, and how customary law affects various issue areas including women's rights and property rights.

EXPERIENTIAL RELEVANCE

One of the challenges of the study of African customary law is the experiential relevance of the individual studying the legal type. I have observed a demarcation between African scholars and Africanists. African scholars are scholars who are of African descent and have firsthand experience participating in customary law, while Africanists are any scholars who focus on Africa. The two camps, in my experience, usually do not have enough interaction. In the African sections of the top policy and political science conferences only 5 percent of the presenters are of African descent or have long-term experience on the African continent. Such an observation does not imply bias, but the reality of the demarcation in the study of customary law. As Bennett (1991) argues, "few, if any, texts on customary law can claim to be direct, personal accounts of community practice" and furthermore, "most who write on the subjects are not part of these communities but work as informants, thus their work bears the preconceptions and prejudices" (1). My direct personal participation with sub-Saharan customary law should help ameliorate part of the deficit of direct experience in the case of my research. I was born and raised in Eastern Africa and have taken part or been witness to customary law processes such as initiation and marriage. In addition, as a social scientist trained in the scientific method, I am able to bring scientific objectivity and methods that allow for empirical examination, while also bringing in a body of theory that allows me to make informed hypotheses that are not just normatively or policy driven.

PRINCIPLE VERSUS CUSTOM

Another salient issue on the topic lays in the very mis-conceptualization of the legal type as "customary" law which distorts our understanding on the difference between a mere custom and customary law. For instance, I have heard presenters assert that female genital mutilation (FGM) or female circumcision is nothing more than a mere custom. I consider such a viewpoint a part of the Austinian handicap because if circumcision is nothing more than a simple custom, how has it continued despite numerous international and domestic policies and laws aiming to stop it. I argue the main problem has been the focus on acts of customary law rather than the understanding of the principles. For instance, in groups like the Maasai, the principle of the rights of passage where a young person moves from childhood to young adulthood which follows the same principle as the Jewish bar mitzvah for boys and bat mitzvah for girls, encompassed circumcision. Therefore, it is possible to keep the principle while modifying the act or the manifestation of that particular principle. The lack of understanding the difference between principles and acts has led to repressing groups who then build a resistance against those who are viewed as attempting to destroy deeply reverenced principles. Bennet (1991) asserts that the Austinian handicap was started during the colonial era with European legal practitioners who viewed customary law as simple primitive "pre-law" customs not worthy of legal examination. To properly assess customary law, I argue that one has to understand that it is a legal type that consists of principles and acts. The atoms of law are principles which are the ideas and precepts, while the acts are the actions that follow or are associated with the principles. Principles emerge from repeated and accepted rules, norms and customs in a society. When a principle bears a level of sanction in society it is framed into a law.

In 2016, I had the privilege of traveling to Nairobi, Kenya and lecture a graduate course. An interesting debate that once came up in the classroom was between the students who believed in the right to female circumcision, while another group denied its legitimacy and referred to the act as female genital mutilation, FGM. In part, I understood the issue that the students confronted. What were the proponents in the classroom really arguing? Was it for the act or was it against legal repression? Were they simply backward barbarians and heathens in need of deliverance and indoctrination, or did they have a deeper intrinsic fear of outsides trying to alter their laws that gave them a sense of identity? In such salient cases, it is important to understand the difference between principles and acts in order to bring equity to the modification of laws.

As early as the 1980s, the government of Kenya had banned FGM, but many ethnic societies continued with the act because people cannot simply legislate or use coercive action to change societal laws. Currently, the Kenyan government and community organizers have come to a better understanding of the difference between principles and laws. Instead of using force, they decided to work alongside communities that practiced circumcision as a part of the rights of passage and alter the act from circumcision to training courses (Dept of Justice 2017, Reid 2017). The government realized that it could change the acts that manifest a law while preserving the principles in law that give people their sense of collective identity. This is important, because the principle behind FGM may be different in other countries. For instance, while FGM is becoming extinct in Kenya, in neighboring Somalia UNICEF estimates 98 percent of women undergo circumcision (Washington Post 2018). I had a conversation with an old Somali Elder who asserted that for his ethnic society they practiced an extreme form of circumcision which began as a result of raiding groups who would raid villages and rape women.

So, for them, the act of circumcision follows completely different principles; therefore, understanding this one can approach the community and discuss the reality that raider groups no longer exist and therefore the basis of the act no longer has standing in that particular clan. In turn, you can get into deliberation with elders to nullify the laws that may have no basis because both the principles and acts may no longer be viable versus Kenya where you change the act but preserve the principle of rites of passage in some of the ethnic societies. Another example of the modification of customary law can be seen even in other parts of the world. Kimberely Motley, an American lawyer who went to Afghanistan and legally aided women and poor, discussed how she went to Afghanistan and worked through a Jurga or a traditional court to prove that a young girl sold into marriage violated not only the constitutional law of the country, but also violated the customary law. She further asserted that those who cause injustice in customary law usually violate the laws of the country and the customary laws themselves. As with the Kenyan government, Motley went to the citizens who adhered to customary law and was able to work with the people to modify law and make corrections where law was wrongly applied. I refer to this process as the positive modification of law, where we can modify law while considering the underlying principles and acts. As NAS law remains one of the most important and quintessential forms of political and social organization in Africa, its modification requires a proper understanding of its origins and principles.

GLOBAL LEGAL EXPECTATIONS VERSUS CUSTOMARY LAW

Another salient area in the study of the legal type is the policy preference of international treaty bodies. When analyzing global trends some perceive that it is an error to assert that liberal global norms are anti–customary law and that a high level of provisions for customary law in state constitutions would be an anomaly. I argue that when we observe the top treaty bodies, they deviate from African customary law models. The Human Rights Committee, the Committee on the Elimination of Discrimination against Women (CEDAW), and the International Convention on Civil and Political Rights (ICCPR) all argue for the removal or altering of customary law, especially on family and marriage which are the two main areas that customary law covers. For instance, the ICCPR Article 3, the CEDAW Gen. Rec. 21, Para. 14, and CEDAW Gen. Rec. 29.M all argue for the removal or altering of polygamy as a viable form of marriage (UN Women Endvawnow 2012). At the same time, we observe a deviation in the continent with the enduring prominence of customary law which is no more evident than in the promulgation of the new 2014 Marriage Act by the Kenyan legislature that protects the institution of customary marriages which encompasses the protection of polygamy. This, in turn, is further affirmed in Article 45 (4) of the new 2010 Kenyan Constitution that provides for different types of marriages, including customary marriages. The new marriage act not only deviates from the expected liberalized global norms against polygamy, but also illustrates the importance of customary law in the sub-Saharan region. Customary law principles deviate from liberal Western and internationalist principles. When then President Obama visited Kenya in 2015, he argued for the right of anyone to marry whomever they wished, and right after he finished his speech the Kenyan President, Uhuru Kenyatta, took the podium and argued that such a viewpoint was a non-issue in the country, indicating politely that such legal principles were not only foreign but not part of the African legal identity. African policy makers are pushing back by arguing for the exclusivity of heterosexual marriages while supporting the merits of polygamy. Such differentiations in legal principles does warrant more scholarly examination.

Reconciling international standards with NAS law creates a tension between universalism and cultural relativism. For instance, the CEDAW, Article 16 clause 1, argues for the right to equality in a marriage, including the right to choose a family name. In addition, the CEDAW also argues for the same rights for both spouses in respect of the ownership, acquisition, management, administration, enjoyment, and disposition of property. International law, in part, works to change extremely salient areas in the African family relations. Ashenafi (2003) asserts that NAS law should conform to the state constitution or nullification should occur if it contradicts the constitution. However, international law tends be pro-Western law and philosophy which at times does not consider the differing legal traditions.

I remember teaching an African studies course in the U.S. where the question of circumcision also came up; however, the question was whether male circumcision was legally equal to that of the women. One of my students argued vehemently that he had read African men needed to be circumcised to reduce their ability to catch diseases, justifying male circumcision over that of women. I have to admit that I found the argument rather arrogant due to the fact that the whole proposition was based on the assumption that circumcision in the sub-Saharan setting was to assist sub-Saharans with a hygiene issue. The reason I disagreed with such assumptions is the fact that if hygiene were the main reason, we would assume circumcision would occur when a boy is a toddler when hygiene really matters but, in fact, it is a rite of passage that occurs during young adulthood. The student was justifying an action based on his experience and biased research that contrasted with that of the African experience. What was not understood is that a significant number of sub-

Saharan men do not get circumcised due to their customs, and that those who do, wait until they are in their teens. Therefore, if health was the reason, then why wait, and wouldn't that mean that most African men should have died of diseases before their teenage years? In part, this is why empirical studies are crucial where we can test data against arguments. A balance should be met in improving NAS law and not marginalizing it to Western centric or globalized sentiments. Bennett (1991) argues that different types of law can inform each other in order for each law to evolve. An-Na'im (2003) argues, that "at one level the forcible displacement of NAS law which is more culturally relevant and accessible in exchange for a colonial legal system that is much maligned constitutes a human rights violation in itself" (25). He further asserts that statutory law lacks the capability of serving the urban population, let alone the rural population without providing these populations with access to the legal apparatus. Therefore, the challenge is with the process of understanding and modifying NAS law according to its principles.

DEFINING CUSTOMARY LAW

An opportunity area in the study of customary law is in the definition of the legal type. The literature has no single agreed upon definition in literature of this legal type (Cuskelly 2011; Bennett 1991; Allott 1984; White 1965; Fortes and Evans-Pritchard 1940). Therefore, I add to the conversation by conceptualizing and reframing customary law as neo-autogenous sub-Saharan (NAS) law to provide a better understanding of its origins, to develop a stronger foundation for a definitional framework, and to acknowledge that NAS law is a discrete form of law. I argue that customary law is "autogenous" or independently emerging out of the sub-Saharan legal experience. I also delineate it as "neo" due to external influencing factors like colonization. I recognize that there are other regions of the world that have their own neo-autogenous laws (NAL); however, I will not be able to examine the breadth of the global autogenous legal types in this book. In addition, I provide a rich understanding of customary law by doing a comparative constitutional examination of the law. In the same way scholars examine constitutional rights provisions like the right to vote, I examine customary law provisions in state constitutions. Of course, one can question why I privilege constitutional provisions over statutory law. On that argument, I do agree that examining statutory law is important; however, so is the examination of constitutional provision because constitutions are norm setters, and after 50 to 60 years post-independence, I assert that it is important to start examining the effect of constitutional legal norms in sub-Saharan states. Therefore, it is not a one or the other preference because scholars should examine both constitutional and statutory laws, and in this book, I primarily focus on constitutional law. I add to customary law research by creating an original quantitative data set. Specifically, I read and code all provisions for customary law in sub-Saharan state constitutions and amended constitutions from 1955 through 2013. From the data I have collected, I find an increase over time in provisions that delineate the protection of customary law, in part, demonstrating an increase in importance of the legal or type on the continent.

CONSTITUTIONAL PROVISIONS FOR CUSTOMARY LAW

Another opportunity that scholars have is in the examination of the legal protection and status of the law in state constitutions. There is a rich constitutional history of sub-Saharan states engaging customary law. For instance, in the 1970s and 1980s, we see constitutions that banned customary law. Mondlane (2003), who sat on Mozambique's Constitutional Council which is the highest body on constitutional and electoral law in Mozambique, argues that there was an abolishing of traditional authority in 1975 because it was associated with colonial oppression. Through my research I was able to find the 1975 Mozambique Constitution and in Article 4, the constitution asserts, "The People's Republic of Mozambique has the following fundamental objectives: the elimination of colonial and traditional structures of oppression and exploitation and the mentality that underlies them." Another example is the 1967 Uganda Constitution. Article 118 asserts,

> (1) The institution of King or Ruler of a Kingdom or Constitutional Head of a District, by whatever name called, existing immediately before the commencement of this Constitution under the law then in force, is hereby abolished. (2) Notwithstanding any provision of this Constitution, the immediately preceding clause shall have effect from 24th May, 1966, in relation to the Kingdom of Buganda. (4) Notwithstanding any provision of this Constitution, Parliament may make provision for the devolution of any property held by any person to whom clause (1) of this article applies by virtue of his office or by any other person or authority, being property connected with or attaching to the institution of King, Ruler or Constitutional Head.

Despite the bans in some states, presently, even in the countries that had once banned customary law, new constitutional amendments and statutory laws have been passed to provide greater protections for customary law. Most recently, President Yoweri Museveni of Uganda pushed for legal recognition of the monarchies and their territories which were once banned in the 1967 constitution. My data demonstrates almost half of sub-Saharan state constitutions have provisions protecting customary law which will be examined in greater detail in chapter 2. Having such a significant number of countries with provisions protecting customary law, including those which had once banned customary law, demonstrates that the topic is worthy of empirical examination. Therefore, the core of my book is an empirical constitutional comparative work. An-Na'im (2003), the Charles Howard Candler Professor of Law at Emory Law, asserts that the majority of the states in sub-Saharan Africa practice and recognize customary law in their legal systems, either directly or indirectly. He further argues that, "at one level the forcible displacement of customary law which is more culturally relevant and accessible in exchange for a colonial legal system that is much-maligned constitutes a human rights violation in itself" (25). An-Na'im (2003) adds that the appropriate challenge lays in regulating the application of customary law while protecting rights.

My book does not claim to have the singular view of customary law, whether negative or positive. In dealing with the subject, I have found pushback from internationalist and human rights proponents when empirical evidence demonstrates that customary law improves certain rights. On the other hand, in areas where findings argue for the need to modify certain aspects of the law, I received equal pushback from proponents of customary law who assume that I wish to discredit or argue for the removal of customary law. What my book aims to do is to give an honest examination of customary law by examining the definitional framework of customary law, examining the debates surrounding the law, and finally, doing rigorous empirical analyses on the topic. I recommend that proponents of the law should allow for checks where warranted, and along the same lines, critics should also accept empirical findings that demonstrate positive impacts of the legal type even if they do not follow their desired policy goals to better improve on the scholarship and policies. When examining the future of the law in sub-Saharan Africa, I argue that customary law, as a discrete legal type, will continue to play an intricate role in shaping the future of sub-Saharan Africa's social, political and legal landscape. I recommend that all parties examining customary law should have greater intersectionality in approaching the topic. While there are areas where customary law should be modified as with any other legal type, scholars and practitioners should approach customary law as a legal form that can add value to the future of sub-Saharan Africa. I hope to generate conversation between those who are for and against customary law by providing normative debates and data-driven evidence, while encouraging discourse on the study of customary law.

THE BOOK OUTLINE

In the next chapter, I first do a normative examination of customary law to move toward a strong definitional framework of customary law. I also create an original and the first quantitative data set for customary law constitutional provisions (to my knowledge). I perform several descriptive analyses on how sub-Saharan states have dealt with NAS law in their state constitutions. In subsequent chapters, I examine how customary law affects property rights as it pertains to land rights. I examine two perspectives—the individualist perspective arguing for a one-state regulation system and the removal of customary law tenure, and the communalist perspective arguing for a plural tenure system that includes customary law tenure. I do a quantitative examination of customary law's effect on property and find support for the communalist perspective. My study suggests caution on the push toward a one state-led statutory tenure law system. In addition, I examine customary laws relation to women's rights attainment. I examine two differing schools of thought; the critical perspective that argues customary law reduces women's political attainment versus the positive perspective that assert customary law can improve women's political attainment. I do a quantitative examination on how customary law affects women's rights attainment and my analysis suggests a more nuanced understanding when examining the interaction between customary law and women's rights. My findings show that customary law limits women's entrance to political office; however, when controlling for the interaction between democratization and customary law, colonial legacy rather than customary law leads to the marginalization of women's entrance to political office.

Chapter Two

Conceptualizing Customary Law

The first question I usually ask students when lecturing a law and courts course is, "What is law?" It is amazing looking at their stunned faces that stare back at me not knowing how to answer. Law is a concept used in popular culture, a topic discussed in classrooms, and an issue area of discourse in political and news cycles. The debate of law and its emergence has been part of the human experience from Aristotle to Kant. I find explanations of law biased by one's historical context whether conqueror or conquered, political ideology and educational system. At the very basic level, I assert that law is a tool of societal order. I deviate from the argument that society is not the coming together of individuals to protect property; rather it is growing out of families who create laws to bring order. As the expansion of families progresses, societies form and with increased proximity between societies, some are engrafted into the larger societies while those of similar size and strength form treaties or have conflicts. I find four different paths that have led to the modern state. In the first path, two societies that have similar characteristics choose to move further away to avoid chaos. In the second path, the two societies choose to coexist by signing treaties or agreements on how to live together in an orderly and peaceful way. In the third path, the two societies go to battle where one wins and takes over or a stalemate occurs and they sign a treaty reverting to the second path. Finally, in the fourth path, which occurred in most of the colonized world, a conquering society colonizes several societal states and groups them into colonized territory. At independence, the conquering state fashions the colonized territory into a state that mirrors that of the colonizing state. Sub-Saharan customary law exists within states where a conquering state colonized several societal states and grouped them into colonized territories. At independence, these colonized territories that encompassed different societal states gained independence, giving birth to the modern African state.

While I find that we can learn from best practices on the study of law, not having an understanding of sub-Saharan principles can skew not only the development but the understanding of what customary law is. Fortes and Evans-Pritchard (1940) assert theories of political philosophy do not adequately further our understanding of the African political systems because they explain how and under what regime types people ought to live, rather than explaining their actual political habits and institutions. Likewise, I argue that examining the formation of law without understanding African principles has led to the inability to properly define the law. Current studies of law emerged from non-African legal perspectives which bear implications on our understanding of NAS law and its place in modern society. I categorize two particular perspectives that analyze the emergence of law: 1) the positivists perspective arguing that law emerges from a prism usually a sovereign "king" which led to a view that NAS law is a lesser law, and 2) the organic view of law asserting that law emerges from the bottom up as people interact in society, which agrees with a plural legal existence in a state. The dominant perspective during colonization was the positivist perspective that argued laws flow from the top down with fundamental truths at the top of social order following a system of deduction. The philosopher Hegel (1812, 1816) argued that laws emerge from the top where one finds or discovers truth *a posteriori*, where after observation and analyzing, the subject repeats the predicate of established law, not its discovery. In other words, the governing state organs create law and pass down the law to citizens, who then act upon those laws and regulations. Positivists stand against relativism and individuality of legal thought outside the bounds of the state. To the colonial powers, the hierarchical formation of law according to positivism translated to the King and his legislature creating rules and passing those rules down to the subjects. Due to the fact that sub-Saharan first nations did not resemble European states, positivists during the colonial era erroneously asserted that all African societies were acephalous, without executives, where decision making was through consensus versus through a state government. In turn, colonial legal scholars asserted that laws and institutions found in sub-Saharan Africa were not worthy of rigorous academic examination (Bennett 1990). Such a generalization of the sub-Saharan legal and political experiences ignored the many Kingdoms, Chiefdoms and democratic formations that existed on the continent prior to colonial conquest (Forde and Kaberry Ed. 1967; Davidson 1965; Bradbury 1967).

On the other hand, the organic perspective asserts that the people carve out their own rules, and over time those rules grow deeply embedded in the fabric of their community and social lives, and presumably, carry much more legitimacy. The philosopher Ehrlich (1912), in his *Fundamental Principles of the Sociology of Law,* argued that the state does not have to create law; rather, rules rely on the association of people. Sheleff (2000) asserts that "social life is dependent on the capacity of people to create rules to guide them in their everyday activities and these rules represent a common denominator which may be enumerated in different ways by retroactive announcements of adjudication, general acknowledgment and, acceptance of agreed and known norms of behavior" (1). The organic formation of law argues for social pluralism where different associations coexist with their own rules bringing the acceptance of a variety of political and legal formations. Bennett (1991, 1) argues that studies of law should analyze three core questions: 1) why does a particular rule develop in the way that it did, 2) how does a law relate to the social, political and economic changes occurring in a particular society, and 3) what interpretation of the law allows for expression of individual rights and freedoms. In the context of sub-Saharan Africa, he also argues for the importance of examining the current understanding of NAS law and its intersection with pre-colonial and European colonial influences. In this chapter, I work to phrase and conceptualize customary law as "neo-autogenous Sub-Sahara African law" or in short form NAS law. Autogenous means "emerging out of" (appropriate here because the majority of NAS law emerged from the indigenous sub-Sahara population), and the qualifier, "neo" denotes "revived" or "modified" (appropriate here because of external influences mostly from colonial experience, that modified NAS law). I argue for the importance of conceptualizing customary as "neo-autogenous law" for several reasons including 1) it provides a better understanding of NAS law origins, 2) it provides a strong foundation for a definitional framework and 3) it acknowledges NAS law as a discrete form of law from other legal or types. NAS law originates significantly from domestic sources because prior to colonization Africans had their own societies with their own autogenous systems and laws. Europeans observing the systematic rules, institutions and legal actions of the African people referred to their systems as customary law. I assert NAS law has its own base principles and does not cease to be its own discrete legal type even if subsequently codified.

In this chapter, I provide a normative analysis of NAS law, and then work to conceptualize the law. After, I analyze NAS law provision in state constitutions by creating an original and the first quantitative data set on NAS law provision (to my knowledge). More specifically, I read and coded constitutional provisions recognizing and protecting NAS law in sub-Saharan state constitutions for all sub-Saharan states for the years 1952 to 2013.

THE BIFURCATED STATE

The African colonial experience brought about bifurcated state formations where indigenous legal and political formations continued to exist alongside the colonial systems. Furthermore, the colonial legacy of having bifurcated states continued long after independence. Mamdani (1996) argues that the indigenous African populations were governed by the autogenous governments in the local state and the heads of these autogenous governments were supervised by white colonial officials creating a two-tiered structure with the autogenous government coexisting alongside the colonial government. In present-day Africa, An-Na'im (2003) asserts that a majority of the states in sub-Saharan Africa practice and recognize NAS law in their legal systems, either directly or indirectly. Many similarities exist in NAS law across sub-Saharan Africa, especially laws concerning land and family. The prevalence of NAS law continues: for instance, former South African President Jacob Zuma of South Africa has six wives, the revered statesman Nelson Mandel was not only a president but was also a member of the Thembu royal family, and in Ghana there is the Ashanti King, and the states of Lesotho and Swaziland are monarchies adhering to NAS law. Chimhowu and Woodhouse (2006) assess that a large percentage of land in Africa remains under communal or NAS tenure. Likewise, Seafield (2003) argues that despite the lack of strong legal recognition, three-quarters of South Africa's population adheres to NAS law in their domestic affairs. In the same lines, Sewanaya and Awori (2003) assert that NAS law provides primary reference for the regulation of the lives of most Ugandans with respect to basic activities and relationships, including family life and property rights (396). In sub-Saharan Africa, NAS law continues to affect many policy areas including family and women status, property tenure law and political formations. However, as argued by White (1965) and Cuskelly (2011), the literature on NAS law has no single agreed-upon definition. I argue customary law is "autogenous" meaning emerging from the majority of the population, and it is also "neo" or modified through external influences—mostly colonial influence.

RELATIONSHIP BETWEEN NAS LAW AND COLONIAL INHERITED LAW

Understanding the relationship between NAS law and colonial inherited law, which forms most of the statutory law, is central to the formal study of NAS law because of the difference in social paradigms, including the importance of the individual versus the community and the right to equality versus the right to cultural norms. Gahamanyi (2003) argues that the tension between the two legal systems primarily lies in matters that deal with an individual's status, lineage, and inheritance. Ashenafi (2003) asserts that the problem in reconciling state law and NAS law lies primarily in tension between the right to equality and the right to cultural norms. For example, Ashenafi argues, "while the Ethiopian constitution guarantees the equality of all persons, most religious and NAS laws do not treat women and men equally" (36). In a similar argument, Seafield argues that constitutional provisions which recognize NAS law bring confrontation between two opposing principles—individual rights versus collective rights. (307)

Tom Mboya, a former leader in the Kenyan independence movement and minister of justice and constitutional affairs, summarized the issues between NAS law and inherited colonial law during the 1958 All Africa People's Conference right before independence,

> We concluded that, if government tried to destroy tribal culture and customs, language and ethnical groupings, they would create such a vacuum that the African might find he had nothing to stand upon and become a most bewildered person in the modern world . . . no effort was made to trace what was good, or point out to potential leaders of a community how some customs could be modified to suit the changes in the world . . . Africans were simply taught European social behavior and the way European workmen live their lives, without any reference to African customs. . . . The question is whether we can develop within Africa a system which reflects the African personality but is at the same time a growing system. (63–64)

The 1958 All Africa People's Conference, that Mboya participated in, demonstrated the importance and challenges of forming states with legal systems that have differing cultural and legal experiences. According to Mboya, the conference articulated the need of maintaining NAS law while also realizing the law would conflict with colonial inherited law. Mboya also stated that the conference realized that these two conflicting legal traditions created the need for a legal framework in which NAS law could evolve and modernize. However, from independence forward, the tension between NAS law and statutory law has not subsided.

While state action has tended to suppress NAS law relative to statutory, some pushback to this suppression has emerged in the courts. For example, Gahamanyi (2003) asserts that despite subordination of NAS law, the courts actually give it precedent in some areas in order to alleviate the harsh effect of state law, especially in regard to affiliation and inheritance. He further states that in Rwanda, parties resist changes made to NAS law when the parties see the change as harmful. In addition, Ashenafi (2003) asserts that a significant segment of the population in Ethiopia supports legal recognition for NAS laws and among the reasons for resistance is that statutory law at times may seem unreasonable and harsh to the population. For example, Mondalane (2003) reports that in Mozambique burning a $200 hut may result in a 15-year prison sentence for arson under civil law; but under NAS law the perpetrator would pay reparations by rebuilding one or two huts (194). Gahamanyi (2003) argues that Rwandan statutory law labelled a child born from an adulterous relationship an "adulterine." Adulterines are then shunned in society; however, NAS law considers that same child the offspring of the mother and her husband.

Lastly, reconciling NAS and statutory laws presents additional difficulties by trying to resolve two different legal paradigms. For instance, NAS law's emphasis on restorative justice contrasts with statutory law's emphasis on punitive justice. Gahamanyi (2003) asserts that under retributive European law, crimes are resolved through punishment, while under NAS law, crimes are addressed through reparations and reconciliation, with the exception of severe crimes such as murder and treason. In addition, Gahamanyi argues that conflicting legal paradigms exist in family law, for example, when dealing with matters on inheritance for children from polygamous marriages that are not easily addressed under statutory law. For example, he asserts that the constitution of Rwanda abolished NAS polygamy in 1950; however, NAS law marriage (which includes polygamy) continued until 1988, which created legal confusion to the population. In addition, An-Na'im (2003) asserts that Western liberal norms emphasizing political and civil rights, while disregarding economic, social and cultural or collective rights have become the norm of some African constitutions brings tensions within sub-Saharan societies (17). Therefore, I assert that without a strong conceptualization, studying the subject becomes challenging for scholars.

Table 2.1. Comparing NAS Law and Colonial Inherited Law Across Salient Characteristics

Neo-autogenous Law	*Statutory Law*
Communal	Individual
Restorative Justice	Punitive Justice
Cultural Relativism	International Universalism

TOWARD A CONCEPTUALIZATION

The conceptualization of customary law as NAS law is especially important for scholars and those who have no familiarity with sub-Saharan legal formations. In addition, customary law exists within bifurcated states due to both colonization and the transition to independent states. However, I argue customary law as a term does not properly serve to help the scholar nor the student in properly understanding this legal type. Therefore, I first examine the characteristics of NAS law, different perspectives on the emergence of law, and work to add to the study of customary law by conceptualizing the law as neo-autogenous sub-Saharan law.

NAS LAW ACCORDING TO ITS CHARACTERISTICS

One of the common ways of conceptualizing NAS law emphasizes examining customary law's characteristics. Bennett (1990) argues that scholars have more interest in examining the characteristics of customary law than in analyzing its exact definition, which may be due to a lack of familiarity with the principles of the law, thus scholars cannot properly define the law and simply define it as the uncodified law of small-scale communities (White 1965; Allott 1984; Bennett 1991). For instance, Fortes and Evans-Pritchard (1940) examine two different structural characteristics found in autogenous societies—those that are centralized and those that are decentralized. However, it is good to note that examining NAS law according to its characteristics at times lacks generalizability because a limited geographic perspective may bias researchers' perceptions of the law. Despite that fact many small rural communities practice NAS law, many other larger communities, like the Agikũyũ (10 million) and the Yoruba (40 million), who have populations in the millions, also practice the legal type.[1]

From the literature and my internal knowledge of NAS law, several characteristics seem to be prevalent that can be observed in Table 2.1. First, NAS law has stable principles, for example, rites of passage and initiation (Bennett 1991). Second, the law follows distinct traditional ethnic lineages through blood or marriage relations (Bohannan 1952). These laws emerge and pass on as a part of ancestral heritage and kinship ties, and thus usually pertain to a select ethnic association. Third, NAS law may affect members' lives in regard to gender status, family relation, and property rights to varying degrees, depending upon factors like marital and social status (Chimhowu and Woodhouse 2006; Joireman 2007; An-Na'im Ed. 2003). Fourth, NAS law passes on mostly orally without codification through legal and social interactions, making it more malleable (White 1965; Allot 1985). Fifth, the law coexists with the statutory law of the state (Sheleff 2000). Sixth, distinguished from mere daily customs, NAS law endures across time in legal principle and doctrine (Bennett, 1991).

Table 2.2. Characteristics of NAS Law

Aspect	*Characteristic*
Foundation	Based on stable neo-autogenous principles
Time Limit	Continuous principles long time period
Parties	Practiced by distinct blood & marriage ethnic lineages
Jurisdiction	Property, marriage, rites of passage, gender, communal
Form	Usually not codified
Status	Coexists with other state law but not engrafted

THE SUB-SAHARAN LEGAL EXPERIENCE

The sub-Saharan legal experience was that of colonial powers who were positivists in orientation. Bennett (1991) argues that colonialists used the positivist perspective which was the popular method of understanding and studying law in late nineteenth and early twentieth century in colonial Africa, drastically affecting the development and understanding of NAS law (1-8). He asserts:

> At a time that was critical for its formulation and development, customary law was being applied by people who had a peculiarly narrow view of law. [The main legal emphasis was] that lawyers should concern themselves exclusively with the study of [colonial] law. In consequence a precise definition of law was essential to demarcate the appropriate area of study. And here Austin's simple pronouncement was decisive: law was a rule laid down by a sovereign or political superior. If the acephalous societies of Africa did not fit the political model implied, then it followed that they had no law. This so-called "Austinian handicap" stigmatized customary law as a lesser normative order, and gave lawyers an excuse to abandon it to missionaries and anthropologists. (3)

According to the Austinian handicap, the sovereign commands law and the individual must conform to the state (in translation, since indigenous sub-Saharan states did not have law organized in the European state model, they did not have any law) (Morris 1995: 335–363; Bennett 1991). Bennett (1991) asserts that according to the Austinian handicap, African societies were acephalous where decision making was through consensus versus through a sovereign. Therefore, they had no law as the sub-Saharan system did not fit the implied European political model. Conceptualizing customary law from a positivist's perspective would not consider customary law as a discrete law as it emerges absent the modern European state model. Therefore, at times customary law is framed as primitive law practiced by legally undeveloped groups from such a perspective. Such narrative has impeded customary law's conceptualization by giving it a subordinate status unworthy of academic examination. Therefore, customary law is viewed as inferior to the dominant colonial inherited law. According to Bennett (1991),

> A more pervasive problem, which has never been completely overcome, was an intrinsically ethnocentric bias. This was responsible for the belief that western European society represents the apogee and goal of all development, a belief that conveniently endorsed the racial prejudices of imperial powers. Although evolutionism was later discredited by functionalist anthropology, it survived in popular thinking, and long after it had lost any plausibility in academic circles, it continued to influence thinking in the colonial administration (9).

As argued before, most of sub-Saharan Africa followed the fourth path to the modern state where a strong power conquers several sovereign societal states, organizes them under a colonial territory and the territory becomes referred to as a state. The very delineation of the term "customary" creates the perception that NAS law is nothing more than mere daily customs with the assumption that customs move toward becoming laws (Sheleff 2000). The framing of NAS law as merely customs then itself perpetuates the perception that the law is a type of "pre-law" in the process of becoming a type of "law"—thus, giving it a subordinate status. Sheleff (2000) argues that "custom" implies a lower degree of law than simply "law." The perception of customary law as a prelaw moving toward becoming law clashes with the African legal experience. In sub-Saharan Africa, no legal evolution took place *per se*–rather colonial masters grouped different societies into states and implemented their legal systems with little acknowledgement of African legal principles within statutory law and colonial law was imposed as superior to NAS law.

Historically, colonialists regulated the role of NAS law. Subsequently, these regulations persist in the current constitutions (Sheleff 2000; Allott 1984; An-Na'im 2003; Obiagwu and Odinkalu 2003). Colonizers normally restricted NAS law in two key ways: 1) it could not conflict with the written law of the colonizer and 2) it could not be repugnant to justice, equity, and good conscience. These two restrictions have enduring effects: the first restriction naturally gives the law a subordinate status to other state laws, and the second restriction gives the law a negative connotation. For instance, An-Na'im (2003) argues that according to Ugandan law, the law has to satisfy three tests: 1) proof of applicability to the party claiming it, 2) no repugnance to natural justice, equity and good conscience and 3) no incompatibility either directly or by necessary implication with written law. NAS law was mostly relegated to the local instead of the national. Mahmood Mamdani (1996) argues that "there were three distinctive features about the customary as colonial power came to define it . . . customary was considered synonymous with the tribal; each tribe was defined as a cultural group with its own customary law . . . [it] came to be all-encompassing; more so than in any other colonial experience, it came to include a customary access to land. Third, custom was defined and enforced by customary Native Authorities in the local state backed up by the armed might of the central state." Therefore, in order to conceptualize customary law, we must start by first examining the autogenous formation.

AUTOGENOUS

Prior to colonization, sub-Sahara Africans had their own societies which contained and fostered autogenous systems and laws. The literature supports the existence of legitimate sovereign states in the pre-colonial period (Forde and Kaberry Ed. 1967; Davidson 1965; Ingham 1975; Kent 1970; Lombard 1967; Bradbury 1967; Kenyatta 1965; Barnett and Njama 1966). These first societies and kingdoms had legal systems that structured their economic, social, and political affairs, and maintained their societies. Bradbury (1967) asserts that "in the late fifteenth century the Benin Kingdom was a well-established state with a large army conducting long campaigns far afield [as it was] approaching the peak of its power and prosperity [and] by the late sixteenth century its frontiers had reached out westward along the coast to beyond Lagos" (5). Another example is Lombard (1967) who asserts that the Kingdom of Dahomey had a centralized system with well-defined governmental units which included various ministries.[2] Moreover, Forde and Kaberry Ed. (1967) describe the kingdoms in Western Africa including the Benin dynasty, the Kingdom of Dahomey, the Kingdom of Kom, and the Mossi Kingdoms—all as including indigenous autogenous law. Similarly, Davidson (1965) describes several African empires including Mali, Songhay and Kanem-Bornu with autogenous legal traditions. In addition, Ingham (1975) describes the Kingdom of Toro in West Uganda, Kent (1970) examines the Sakalava Empire of Western Madagascar and, Kenyatta (1965) and Barnett and Njama (1966) describe the laws and the devolved system of the Agikuyu of Kenya.

It is important to note that by the late 1880s, only about five percent of Africa experienced colonization or occupation, and prior to the Berlin Conference of 1884-85, roughly eighty percent of Africa remained under sub-Saharan autogenous laws and systems. The Portuguese and Arabs had influenced the east and west sub-Saharan coastal regions, and the Dutch the southern region earlier; however, the interior of Africa did not have much contact with the outside world before the twentieth century. Colonization of the African continent occurred within a short period, roughly between 1889 and 1920, except for Ethiopia and Liberia, and organized into colonial territories under imperial rulers. European legal traditions of civil and common law began influencing autogenous law (White 1965; Allott 1984; Bennett 1995).

NEO

Neo here refers to the revived or modified nature of autogenous law. The treatment of customary law differed depending on colonial administration—for instance, the British versus the French systems. In this section, I examine two of the dominate colonial types, the British and the French colonial administration. French assimilated autogenous systems to their colonial system whereas the British used indirect rule, a policy led by Lord Lugard the British governor-general of the first united Nigeria. He argued that the best method for the "British administration was by conserving, officially recognizing, and using the existing indigenous systems of rule and law" (Allott 1984: 58). The British allowed autogenous law to coexist with certain core legal caveats. For example, under British rule, autogenous law was not supposed to conflict with the written law of the colonizer or be repugnant to justice, equity, and good conscience. In addition, in cases where there was no central authority, the British imposed chiefs (Crowder 1964: 199). Historically, colonialists regulated the role of autogenous law according to Western legal thought. Subsequently, these regulations persist in the current constitutions (Sheleff 2000; Allott 1984; An-Na'im 2003; Obiagwu and Odinkalu 2003).

The French and British systems were similar in that they both used autogenous leaders to rule; however, the difference was in the position and power of autogenous leaders and their relation to the colonial political officer. According to Crowder (1964), the French did not find autogenous law beneficial and preferred assimilating the indigenous population into French laws and systems. The French used autogenous leaders as agents of the political officer who defined the leaders' duties and powers (199). In contrast, the British aimed to preserve autogenous institutions in their original structures. According to Kane (2003), the French reorganized and subordinated autogenous systems to serve their administrational needs (109). Crowder (1964) asserts that autogenous leadership in the French colony was subservient and colonially driven. The French even rearranged the traditional geographical boundaries originally controlled by autogenous law and turned them into administrative cantons, thus chiefs at times lost control of their original traditional territorial authority.[3] Consequently, the rearrangements and exploitation of NAS law systems in turn made autogenous leaders, law, and institutions very unpopular in French colonies among the colonized population. Crowder (1964) argues that upon gaining independence, states such as Guinea did away with chiefs with little protest from the population (200–201).

The transitional process from colonialism to independent states also differed with the British having major conferences to see how to handle autogenous law within colonies transitioning, while the French provided no support for autogenous law. At the advent of independence, the French did not put any effort into supporting the autogenous institutions like chieftaincy in their colonies. Crowder argues that the French officers, unlike the British who settled in their colonies, left at the advent of independence, leaving administrative gaps. Kane (2003) asserts that French officials in Guinea departed upon independence, causing a major shortage in judicial civil servants and, in turn, the state consolidated all the laws and banned NAS law (109). The British case was different. For instance, the top British judge of the time, Lord Denning, chaired the London Conference on the Future Law in Africa that convened in December 1959 until January 1960. The London Conference examined different areas of law and their relation to autogenous law including tort law, criminal law, contract law and appeals to higher courts. The major conclusion of the conference was that the British desired conformity in criminal law, trade law and commerce law immediately, though in other areas unification was not desirable or practical at that time. In addition, there was also the Dar es Salaam Conference on local courts and autogenous law in Africa in 1963 that focused on areas of reform in NAS law (Allot 1984). The conference resolved that there was a need to reform law, especially on new issues such as bankruptcy, that autogenous law does not address. In addition, the Dar es Salaam Conference pushed for reforms in areas of marriage and inheritance; however, the conference recognized that NAS law would not disappear in the foreseeable future. Thus, the British colonial legacy with indirect rule seems to influence a greater prevalence of autogenous law which may lead to increased provisions in their former colonial territories versus those of the French system of assimilation.

NEO-AUTOGENOUS SUB-SAHARAN (NAS) LAW

NAS law originates significantly from domestic sources, and Europeans examining the systematic rules and legal actions of the African people, referred to these laws as customary. However, the definition does not tell us much about the law nor its origins. The first step in proper conceptualization should be moving away from the view of customary law as a “lesser-law” to viewing it as a unique and discrete type of law practiced to varying degrees by a billion people. NAS law remains the primary system when dealing with family, land and marriage affairs in sub-Saharan Africa and there are many similarities across the continent. Bennett (1991) asserts that studies of law should analyze why a particular law developed in the way that it did in order to properly analyze it. I assert that the proper conceptualization of the law is neo-autogenous sub-Saharan law. It recognizes not only its regional relevance but its historic manifestation on the African continent prior to colonization. Furthermore, it recognizes the reality that sub-Saharans were a legally complex people who had their own states and systems. The conceptualization also recognizes the reality of influence and also asserts, in part, the need of modification. My study therefore adds to the discourse on the subject of NAS law by providing a richer framework.

Some of the literature inaccurately argues that codification causes NAS law to stop evolving in order to reflect the conduct and habits of the people. I argue the counter and assert that NAS law must evolve like other legal types to reflect current realities and challenges. Bennett (1991) asserts that NAS law evolves in the same manner as any other type of law, through judicial review and legislative revisions. Simmance (1961), who examined land redemption among the Fort Hall Kikuyu, found that NAS land laws had evolved in accordance to societal needs. For instance, we find that the constitution of Ghana tasks the House of Chiefs to codify and build upon NAS law in the same manner as any other type of law.

With an improved conceptualization and terming in the study of customary law as neo-autogenous sub-Saharan law, we then can examine the extent of NAS law provisions in sub-Saharan state constitutions. As asserted, constitutions are norm-setters and after roughly 60 years post-independence in most sub-Saharan nations, a comparative constitutional assessment will be of great value in understanding how sub-Saharan states have dealt with the legal type across time. Therefore, I examine the extent of NAS law provisions in sub-Saharan constitutions next.

THE EXTENT OF NAS LAW IN STATE CONSTITUTIONS

Modern state constitutions form the base of a state's legal and political systems. Therefore, if there is a provision for a particular area of law, we can examine the level of attention that area of law is given which, in part, depicts the level of saliency that provision garners in the state. For instance, there are many comparative constitutional studies that examine the number of provisions for individual rights to a public trial or provisions that provide for judicial independence. Along the same lines, I examine constitutional provisions for NAS law by creating an original quantitative measure on NAS law provisions. Specifically, I read and coded constitutional provisions recognizing and protecting NAS law in state constitutions for all 49 sub-Saharan states for the years 1952 to 2013. My measure includes the coding of 196 state constitutions across two descriptive categories—formal constitutional recognition of NAS and recognition of specific NAS law institutions.[4] Examining NAS law provisions is important because a formal recognition of a legal type provides protection to the use of the law and also demonstrates the importance of the law to the state. Analyzing provisions for NAS law makes an important quantitative contribution for scholars and social scientists, and further aids in the empirical examination of how NAS law affects issues such as property and family law. First, I operationalize my measures for NAS law in state constitutions, then I do a comparative examination of the provisions across state constitutions.

OPERATIONALIZING THE EXTENT OF PROTECTION IN CONSTITUTIONS

In my initial reading of sub-Saharan Africa's constitutions, I identified two core types of provisions in these documents: 1) those that formally recognize NAS law and 2) those that protect specific NAS institutions. The reason of identifying these two core types of provision is due to the fact that I do not interpret the constitution, but rather, I report only specific mentions of customary law—for instance, "Constitution, the laws of Gambia consist of e) customary law (Gambia 1996, Article 7)." The first provision helps to analyze whether a mention is positive or negative—in other words, whether a constitution allows for the existence of NAS law or refutes the existence of the law. The other type of provision is important because it demonstrates even greater complexification and protection for the law by actually providing for specific manifestations or institutions of customary law. Therefore, I create a four-point scale to help delineate the level of provision (2, 1, 0, –1), and examples are described below. If a constitution provides for complete protection it receives a score of 2, starting with the year the provision was promulgated and that score changes only if there is a constitutional change or alteration. Due to colonial legacy, NAS law was regulated to not contradict other laws, giving it a secondary status; therefore, a mention that qualifies or regulates NAS law receives a score of 1, starting with the promulgation year. If the constitution has no mention specifying NAS law, it receives a score of 0, and finally, in the case that a constitution specifically mentions a ban on the use of NAS law and/or NAS law institutions, that constitution receives a score of –1.

For constitutional mention of NAS law, I code the level of provision as follows:

2) Full and explicit protection
1) Qualified/Regulated protection
0) No mention of NAS law
–1) Subordination/Ban on NAS law

Below are examples of the coding applied to constitutions in my sample:

(2) Gambi (1996), Article 7- *In addition to this Constitution, the laws of Gambia consist of—(e) customary law so far as concerns members of the communities to which it applies.*

(1) Angola (2010), Article 7–*The validity and legal force of custom which does not contradict the Constitution and does not threaten human dignity shall be recognized.*

(–1) Bans of NAS law mentioned NAS law institutions as shown below or elements of NAS law rather than stating the ban on NAS law specifically.

For constitutional mentions of NAS Law institutions, I code the level of provisions as follows:

2) Full protection of institutions/actors
1) Qualified/Regulated institutions
0) No mention of institutions/actors
–1) Institutional Subordination/ban

Below are examples of the coding applied to constitutions in my sample:

(2) Swaziland Constitution (1968), Article 1 (1)—*Swaziland is a sovereign independent Kingdom and Article 28 and (1) The King of Swaziland is the Head of State.*

(1) Angola (2010) *Article 213–(Autonomous local government bodies) Clause 2–The forms of local government organization shall include local authorities, the institutions of the traditional authorities and other specific forms of citizen participation, under the terms of the law.*

(–1) Uganda Constitution (1967), 118. (1)–*The institution of King or Ruler of a Kingdom or Constitutional Head of a District, by whatever name called, existing immediately before the commencement of this Constitution under the law then in force, is hereby abolished.*

(–1) Rwanda (1962), Article 2—*The Mwami regime is abolished and may not be restored. The Mwami Kigeri V and all his dynasty shall be deprived of their royal prerogatives.*

(–1) Mozambique Constitution (1975), Article 4—*The People's Republic of Mozambique has the following fundamental objectives: the elimination of colonial and traditional structures of oppression and exploitation and the mentality that underlies them.*

DESCRIPTIVE ANALYSIS

My examination of state constitutions reveals a substantive level of protection for NAS law. In addition, my measure demonstrates a significant variation and a significant level of provisions across constitutions and across time. First, I examine whether there are mentions and the level of mentions in state constitutions in Table 2.3. I find that 84 (42.9 percent of my sample) state constitutions provide some level of formal constitutional recognition on NAS law, and at approximately equal levels, 78 (41.8 percent of my sample) state constitutions provide some level of constitutional protection for specific NAS law institutions. In addition, 48.98 percent of the constitutions have either a provision for recognition or institutions, and 33.67 percent of the constitutions have both provisions for recognition and institutions. These findings are quite remarkable due to the fact that the global expected norm would be that most constitutions are moving toward the same liberal type that would exclude protections for NAS law (Go 2003). In part, the level of protection demonstrates the level of use and merits further descriptive analysis on the substantive treatment of how constitutions deal with NAS law, which I analyze next.

Table 2.3. Percent of Constitutional Provisions for NAS law

Category	*Provision*	*No Provision*
Constitutional Recognition	42.9%	57.1%
Protection of Institutions	41.8%	58.2%
Either Recognition or Institutions	48.98%	51.02%
Both Recognition and Institutions	33.67%	66.33%

Table 2.4 reveals a substantively high level of constitutional attention given to the two components, protection and institutions, with significant variation. As shown in Table 2.4, 42.35 percent of the constitutions provide some substantive treatment of NAS law while 57.65 percent of constitutions have no mention of NAS law. Specifically, 1.02 percent of the constitutions have a score of -1 or a provision that bans NAS law, 19.9 percent of the con-

Table 2.4. Constitutional Provisions for NAS law in State Constitutions

Category	*−1*	*0*	*1*	*2*	*Total*
Constitutional Recognition	0	112	40	44	196
Protection of Institutions	4	114	38	40	196
Total	4 (1.02%)	26 (57.65%)	78 (19.9%)	84 (21.43%)	196

2) Full and explicit recognition or protection
1) Qualified/Regulated recognition or protection
0) No mention of NAS law
−1) Subordination/Ban on NAS law and NAS institutions

stitutions have a score of 1 or a moderate level of protection for NAS law, and 21.43 percent of constitutions have a score of 2 or a full and explicit protection for NAS law. These findings on the substantive treatment that NAS law enjoys in sub-Saharan constitutions is important because they demonstrate not only the fact that there are mentions, but there is a deliberate examination of how the law is to operate in the state, showing in part the importance of NAS law. Next, I do an across-time analysis of the substantive changes in state constitutions to analyze whether provisions of NAS law are decreasing or increasing over time.

In Figures 2.1 and 2.2, and Table 2.5, I examine changes over time, by the decade, by examining the mean in the category score ranging from 2 to −1.[5] At the onset of 1960, a majority of sub-Saharan states achieved independence and therefore set to creating a constitution. Examining Figure 2.1, Figure 2.2, and Table 2.5, in the 1960s, the mean during the period is above zero on both categories, which is significant because it demonstrates that from the onset of independence constitutions provided provisions for NAS law at varying levels. However, we see a decrease in the 1970s leading into 1980s, which may be due to revolutions and coups which led to several states banning constitutions and removing protections for neo-autogenous systems. For instance, several states banned NAS law systems including Uganda (1967), Burundi (1975), and Mozambique (1975). However, since the 1990s there has been a significant increase in NAS law protections. The shift in increased provisions may be due to the fact that most of the states transitioned from authoritarian rule to democratic rule, providing windows of political opportunity for proponents of NAS law to argue for greater protections. The 2000s have seen the trend of promulgating new constitutions or heavily amending old constitutions, which has actually led to highest levels of protection than customary law has enjoyed since dependence.

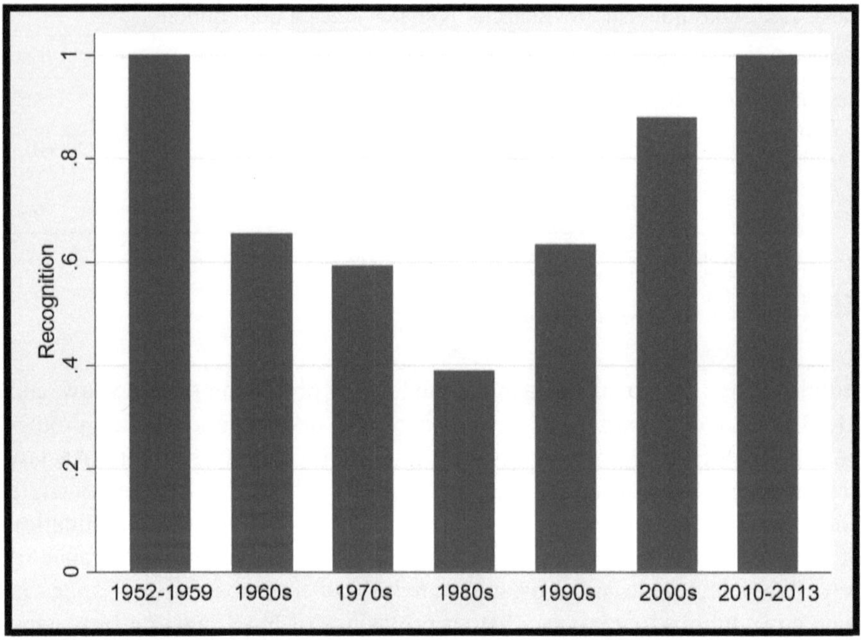

Figure 2.1. Mean of the Constitutional Recognition of NAS Law by Decade

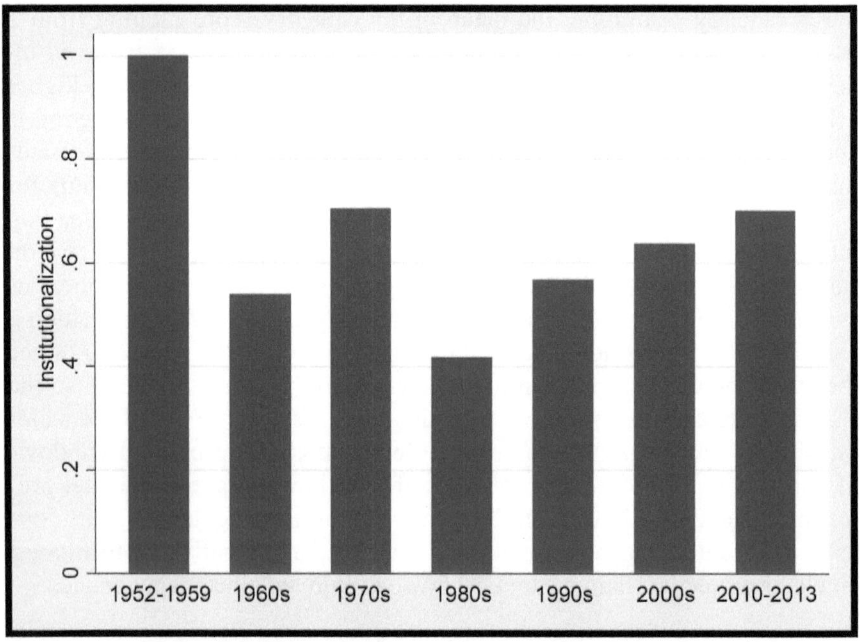

Figure 2.2. Mean of the Protection of NAS Law Institutions by Decade

Table 2.5. Recognition and Institutions by Decade across 196 Constitutions

Constitutional Recognition				*Protection of Institutions*			
Decade	*Mean*	*Std. Dev.*	*Freq.*	*Decade*	*Mean*	*Std. Dev.*	*Freq.*
1952–1959	1	1.2	4	1952–1959	1	1.16	4
1960s	0.7	0.8	26	1960s	0.54	0.99	26
1970s	0.6	0.8	27	1970s	0.7	0.99	27
1980s	0.4	0.8	36	1980s	0.42	0.77	36
1990s	0.6	0.8	60	1990s	0.57	0.75	60
2000s	0.9	0.8	33	2000s	0.64	0.78	33
2010–2013	1	0.8	10	2010–2013	0.7	0.82	10
Total	0.7	0.8	196	Total	0.58	0.83	196

Next, I also descriptively analyze the colonial legacy's relation to NAS law provisions. Turning to colonial legacy, I examine all colonial powers including the most the dominant colonial states of Britain and France. In Table 2.6, all means are above 0, indicating some level of protection for NAS law across all colonial types. As expected, there is a differentiation between the types of colonial administrations and the level of provision that NAS law is provided in state constitutions. As expected, the British colonial legacy has the highest levels of provision, while the French system has the lowest level of provision, which is significant due to the expectation that colonial legacy's effects fade over time (Go 2003). The British colonial legacy has a mean of 1.36 on recognition of NAS law and 1.14 for protection of a specific NAS law institution, demonstrating that former British colonies are associated with high levels of protection of NAS law above the moderate level of qualified/regulated protection. The French legacy mean of recognition for NAS law is 0.11 and the mean of protection for specific NAS law institutions is 0.15, indicating that former French colonies are associated with relatively low levels of protection

Table 2.6. Colonial Legacy Across 196 Constitutions

	Summary of Recognition			*Summary of Institutions*		
Colonial Power	*Mean*	*Std. Dev.*	*Freq.*	*Mean*	*Std. Dev.*	*Freq.*
Britain	1.36	0.77	72	1.14	0.89	72
France	0.11	0.36	79	0.15	0.40	79
Spain	0.83	0.98	6	0.67	1.03	6
Portugal	0.13	0.34	16	0.25	0.68	16
Belgium	0.55	0.52	11	0.27	0.79	11
United States	0.50	0.71	2	1.00	1.41	2
Italy Occupation	0.71	0.95	7	0.71	0.95	7
Germany	0.67	0.58	3	0.67	0.58	3
Total	0.65	0.82	196	0.58	0.83	196

for NAS law. Interestingly, the Spanish, Italian, and German systems have almost a moderate level of provisions with means of approximately 0.75, indicating a qualified/regulated level of protection, while Germany, Belgium, and the United States have means of roughly 0.53, indicating a medium to low level of protection. These descriptive findings signify because they indicate that the colonial legacy depends on the colonial administrative type.

CONCLUSION

The substantive work carried out in this chapter provides not only a rich definitional framework for NAS law, but also provides the reader with a substantive examination of the law's operation in sub-Saharan states. The implications and contributions of my findings are quite vast to both academics and policy makers. The assumption that constitutions are moving toward one-type liberal constitutions or that NAS law is a lesser legal order is significantly contradicted by the presence of NAS law provisions. I set many foundational contributions in the study of sub-Saharan African law.

First, I contribute to sub-Saharan legal literature by providing a richer understanding of customary law by redefining and conceptualizing customary law as neo-autogenous sub-Sahara African law which provides a better understanding of NAS law origins which I demonstrated by showing the rich historical political and legal experience on the continent, providing a strong foundation for a definitional framework by demonstrating the historical evolution of the law and acknowledging NAS law as a discrete form of law from other legal types. Having a strong definitional framework can assist scholars to engage with the subject, especially those who do not have direct engagement with NAS law. As discussed, autogenous means "emerging out of" (appropriate here because the majority of NAS law emerged from the indigenous sub-Sahara population), and the qualifier, "neo" denotes "revived" or "modified" (appropriate here because of external influences mostly from colonial experience, that modified NAS law).

Second, I analyzed the provision for NAS law making an important contribution for human rights scholars, political and policy scientists, and legal scholars who need a richer understanding of how states have dealt with NAS law in order to have a base of understanding when dealing with subjects like property and family law. I contribute to the research on NAS law by creating an original and the first quantitative data set on NAS law provision (to my knowledge). Specifically, I read and coded constitutional provisions recognizing and protecting NAS law in sub-Saharan state constitutions for all sub-Saharan states for the years 1952 to 2013. My data set includes the coding of 196 state constitutions across two descriptive categories—formal constitutional recognition of NAS and recognition of specific NAS law institutions. The statistical analysis provides strong evidence that NAS law is still a significant part of the sub-Sahara legal formation. The findings demonstrate that there are provisions for NAS law recognition and institutions. I find a substantively significant level of provisions that protect sub-Saharan neo-autogenous law, and over time there is a gradual increase in provisions that protect NAS law which, in part, reflects the importance of the legal type on the sub-Saharan continent. Furthermore, there is evidence that the colonial legacy greatly influences how a state interacts with NAS law, probably due to the colonial powers' handling of their colonies and NAS law during the process of decolonization.

These findings have a number of interesting implications for the broader literature, including the reality that NAS law is not only a part of the legal makeup of sub-Saharan Africa, but that the law also receives protection in state constitutions. Overall, my research clearly illustrates that NAS law remains a salient component of sub-Saharan legal pluralism, and strongly suggests that the subject of NAS law merits further consideration by scholars. In my subsequent chapters, I will examine the impact of the national level of tolerance for customary law in two key areas—property transaction costs and women's rights and attainment.

NOTES

1. Central Intelligence Agency, World Fact Book: People and Society, https://www.cia.gov/library/publications/the-world-factbook/.

2. "The centralization of political activity at the capital requires a highly specialized administration. Obviously, the king was not able to cope with the minutiae of government himself. Ministers and officials with well-defined functions dealt with most government business, although they were not permitted to make a final decision on a major question without royal consent. According to Forbes, who visited the capital in the middle of the nineteenth century, the royal retinue consisted of 296 nobles. In effect, however, most power was concentrated in the hands of six high-ranking ministers whose functions were considerably varied" (Lombard 1967: 81).

3. "He [the chief] did not head a local government unit, nor did the area which he administered on behalf of the government necessarily correspond to a pre-colonial political unit. In the interests to conformity, the French divided the state up administratively into cantons that frequently cut across pre-colonial political boundaries . . . Chiefs did not remain chiefs of their old political units but of the new cantons, though sometimes the two coincided. . . . In certain cases, the French deliberately broke up the old political units" (Crowder 1964: 199).

4. In my research, I am measuring NAS law provision in state constitutions, not NAS law practice on the ground.

5. When examining the constitutions that were written in the 1950s, we see only four states because the majority of the states gained independence in the 1960s—Ethiopia, Eritrea, Liberia and Guinea, with Ethiopia and Eritrea driving the mean since Ethiopia was an empire using autogenous law and administratively controlled Eritrea. It is difficult to have confidence in statistics based on an N of 4.

Chapter Three

NAS Law and Property Transaction Costs

Property, as land, remains one of the most salient areas of legal, political and social contention in sub-Saharan Africa. The majority of the sub-Saharan population depend and place a high value on land ownership and occupation. In fact, scholars estimate land held under NAS law tenure constitutes roughly 75 percent of the land (Chimhowu and Woodhouse 2006; Joireman 2008). For example, Zimbabwe and South Africa continue to grapple with controversial issues of land redistribution, and in states like Kenya, issues over land have even played a part in violent political conflicts. In the sub-Saharan ethos, land continues to be tied to communal identity, often sparking the question of how best to handle land under NAS law property tenure.[1] Therefore, in this chapter, I examine property transaction costs in Sub-Saharan Africa that operate under either statutory law tenure or sub-Saharan neo-autogenous (NAS) law tenure.[2] On the question on how to properly handle land, I examine two competing perspectives: the individualist's perspective and the communalist's perspective. As Joireman (2008) notes, "virtually every colonized country had two systems of land holding, one which was regulated by the state and one by customary law and traditional leaders" (9). The main disagreement between the two perspectives lays in the question of finding the most cost efficient and most equitable land tenure system. The individualist perspective argues for exclusive state regulation over property, while the communalist perspective argues for an inclusive plural tenure system. First, I examine the challenge of scarcity leading to higher property transaction costs. I then examine the two competing perspectives, the individualist and communalist perspectives, on land tenure. Finally, I do an exploratory multidisciplinary empirical examination to test what perspectives best work to reduce property transaction costs in sub-Saharan Africa.

SCARCITY AND TRANSACTION COSTS

Sub-Saharan African countries are facing increasing populations which continue to depend on land, leading to scarcity in property. Joireman (2008) argues that "where land is scarce and population densities are higher, land allocation is more contested, [and] conflict over land is more frequent and resort to the courts for dispute settlement and recognition of land transfer is more likely" (13). North (1992) argues that economic growth necessitates setting up efficient political and economic institutions that provide low transaction costs. Transaction costs comprise of the costs incurred while operating an economic system (Libecap1986; North 1992; Joireman 2008). According to Libecap (1986), "transaction costs include the costs of bargaining, information, measurement, supervision, enforcement and political action, and they help to determine how individuals respond to changing economic conditions" (228). Consequently, in sub-Saharan Africa increased scarcity in land has led to higher levels of economic competition. With increased competition, the number of economic transactions has increased, and subsequently, so have the property transaction costs. Increased transaction costs necessitate efficient institutions to mitigate costs, and therefore, I examine different perspectives that speak on land tenure systems.

THE INDIVIDUALIST PERSPECTIVE

I refer to the first perspective as the individualist perspective because it encompasses two arguments: 1) the neo-economist argument with its emphasis on statutory law (one single state law) tenure as the most cost-efficient system in reducing transaction costs (De Soto 1989, 2000; Joireman 2007) and 2) its emphasis on individual ownership over communal ownership (De Soto 1989, 2000). More specifically, individualists argue that property belongs to the individual, not the community. In addition, individualists assert that the individual should enjoy property freely, whether to dispose of the property or keep it to the exclusion of all others, which in turn leads to greater economic and social development. Furthermore, they argue that removing property governance from the purview of NAS land law tenure represents the proper political progress of the modern state. Individualists argue that putting property under one unified state-led statutory law tenure system reduces property transaction costs by encouraging investment and by providing greater security from expropriation. Accordingly, individualists add that through the titling and registering of property, the state 1) improves security, 2) enfranchises women, 3) increases individual capital, and 4) builds credit worthiness (De Soto 1989, 2000; Leblang 1996). Moreover, De Soto (2000) adds that the most appropriate way to help the poor and the disenfranchised is through state-centered property law where the law integrates all property systems into one state-centered social contract on property. In a similar vein, Leblang (1996) asserts that a unified state-centered property law enables the state to 1) measure assets, 2) monitor economic activity, and 3) enforce agreements helping with economic development.

Therefore, individualists would predict that tolerance for NAS law leads to higher property transaction costs. Moreover, individualists argue that the inefficient and inequitable management of property governed under neo-autogenous property law leads to higher transition costs because of uncertainty of ownership with no written contracts, and because of its gendered nature. Joireman (2007) adds that communal tenure has "ambiguity in the definitions and enforcement of land as it pertains to ownership, contract, and land transfer, increasing transaction costs in the exchange [and] transfer [of land]" (465). Likewise, Joireman (2008) asserts that NAS law erodes individual rights, empowers local leaders, undermines democratic institutions, and resists change. Moreover, De Soto (1989) argues that in regard to access to credit, banks would limit or refuse to give loans because of a lack on the guarantee on land ownership under NAS law, short-changing the capital need to invest on the land. Consequently, the individualist's perspective would predict that NAS law provisions lead to higher property transaction costs. From the arguments, we should therefore see a correlation of states with higher levels of NAS law having higher property transaction costs.

The Individualist Hypothesis: States with higher levels of NAS law provision will be more likely to have higher property transaction costs.

THE COMMUNALIST PERSPECTIVE

I refer to the second perspective as the communalist perspective because it encompasses two arguments: 1) that empirical evidence does not support neo-economic claims for the primary expected benefit (reduced property costs) of moving to one state-led statutory law tenure system (Libecap 1986; North 1992), and 2) that communal ownership is a viable alternative to individual ownership (Bennett 1991; Barrow and Roth 1990; Ault and Rutman 1979; North 1992). Communalists argue that institutions do not operate in a vacuum; rather, factors inside and outside the institutions influence transaction costs. Likewise, North (1992) argues that "a zero-transaction-cost model posited by neo-economists does not account for reality" (15). More to the point, communalists argue that empirical evidence does not support the primary expected benefit (reduced property costs) of moving from communal land law to individual land law (Barrows and Roth 1990; Chimhowu and Woodhouse 2006; Ault and Rutman 1979; Dussias 1998; McCulley 2004). Furthermore, they find that the movement from communal land has consequently led to the disfranchisement of the poor and those who do not have the ability to register land. When we turn specifically to delineating property under NAS law, Chimhowu and Woodhouse (2006) argue that communal property law operates according to non-Western market principles, bringing about the greatest complication in the property debate. Instead, NAS property law functions according to the indigenous neo-autogenous perspectives over the control of property. Chimhowu and Woodhouse add that communal lands are compromised primarily of inherited land holdings, while purchased land normally falls outside the boundaries of NAS law. In addition, they assert that ethnic groups maintain property under NAS law practices through lineage, first clearance, settlement, or conquest.[3] For example, the Constitution of Kenya 2010, Article 63 posits that:

> (1) Community land shall vest in and be held by communities identified on the basis of ethnicity, culture or similar community of interest. (2) Community land consists of—(*a*) land lawfully registered in the name of group representatives under the provisions of any law; (*d*) land that is—(i) lawfully held, managed or used by specific communities as community forests, grazing areas or shrines; (ii) ancestral lands and lands traditionally occupied by hunter-gatherer communities; . . . (4) Community land shall not be disposed of or otherwise used except in terms of legislation specifying the nature and extent of the rights of members of each community individually and collectively.

Furthermore, in sub-Saharan Africa, communal property ownership continues to be widely practiced and influences people's livelihoods from land ownership to inheritance. Ault and Rutman (1979) challenge the individualist's perspective on the economic viability of communal ownership by asserting African farmers have capitalistic motivations and do act in a rational manner when responding to economic stimuli during economic changes. They further assert that the images depicting NAS law (i.e. land ownership) as stuck in the nineteenth century world remain inaccurate and biased. Like any other land tenure system, communal tenure in Africa developed in accordance with the rules of economic efficiency by being a flexible code that responds to changing economic conditions. As North (1992) asserts, "the first step in development is to acquire information about the contours of the economy to help identify the costs of transacting and producing, and the institutions that underlie those costs" (17).

As long as transaction costs were positive, sub-Saharans had little incentive to exercise their ownership over land when supply exceeded demand.

However, sub-Saharans exercised their ownership over property once the demand for resources exceeded supply at zero price. Ault and Rutman argue against the erroneous assumptions that land transactions were not common in sub-Saharan Africa prior to colonizers. They assert that just because certain types of transactions did not take place does not mean that the notion of land transactions was unknown, but rather, they assert that instead the local economic and social conditions merely did not warrant individual claim to property. Simmance (1961) demonstrates the ability of NAS law to evolve by identifying land redemption as a specific area in which NAS land law was evolving. Simmance illustrates revisions made on NAS property law by the Fort Hall Kikuyu Council in 1952 on land redemption:

> Land paid as blood money compensation could not be redeemed. When land was redeemed the purchaser could not be ordered to remove his huts. Land which had been bought for ten or more goats, where a ram was slaughtered and matoka lilies planted, could not be redeemed. Land given to a daughter on marriage as ithaga or marriage-gift could be redeemed [but] only by the mutual consent of the parties. Any land, for which ten or more goats had been paid irrespective of whether or not a ram had been slaughtered, could not be redeemable by the vendor against the wishes of the purchaser, although customary refreshers might be demanded. [Finally] all land transactions should in future take place in public, in the presence of Muhiriga [local] representatives from both sides and with the knowledge of all interested persons. (78–79)

Simply stated, Simmance demonstrates that land laws were evolving through revisions and coding. He argues that land redemption, a common land transaction globally, evolved to meet the changing needs of communities in Africa. More specifically, in his examination of land redemption among the Fort Hall Kikuyu of Kenya, he finds that for the Agikuyu, the main reason for the disposal of cultivation land was to pay for offenses or to pay bride prices. In addition, Simmance argues that such disposals were on friendly loan purchases rather than commercial terms, so that purchased land was redeemable by the original owner. However, redemption of land could not take place in certain instances, such as blood payments or public ceremonial disposals. Indeed, communalists do not refute the need for land reform with changing times; rather, they assert that reformers must incorporate NAS property ownership in their reforms because of its importance in the sub-Saharan context. Such consideration becomes necessary for land reforms to work in sub-Saharan Africa (Chimhowu and Woodhouse 2006; Ault and Rutman 1979).

Communalists argue that the consequences of individualist arguments actually hurt a major part of the population dependent on the communal system (Chimhowu and Woodhouse 2006; Barrows and Roth 1990). Titling of land under a one-state tenure was the privilege of the eldest man in a family or clan, leading to the disenfranchisement of youth and women. Moreover, Barrows and Roth (1990) assert empirical evidence does not support the individualists' purported dual benefits of efficient governments and large credit markets through titling as many sub-Saharan states still lack efficient governments and large credit markets. When large traces of communal land were individualized, it was the state government representatives and the elites who frequently accumulated the land by taking the land for themselves. Furthermore, according to Barrows and Roth, in states like Kenya, titling has led to extreme land fragmentation and high litigation cost. Furthermore, they posit that moving away from neo-autogenous tenure has decreased productivity of land, and has consequently led to the disenfranchisement of those who do not have the ability to register land (Barrows and Roth 1990).

The Communalist Hypothesis: States with a higher level of NAS law provision will not be more likely to have higher transaction costs as compared to those with a low level of NAS law provisions.

Next, I empirically test the two competition perspectives on the efficient management property transaction costs.

TESTING THE EFFECT OF NAS LAW ON PROPERTY TRANSACTION COSTS

I engage in an empirical analysis, testing the arguments posited by the two competing perspectives on how NAS law affects property transaction costs. My key data comes from the World Bank Doing Business Project Database (2013). My unit of analysis is county-year for years 2005-2013. The data cover all 49 sub-Saharan states, and I estimate OLS models with continuous dependent variables. The coefficients are interpreted as one unit or percent change in X causes Y to increase or decrease by the reported coefficient. Due to my split audience, those with quantitative backgrounds and without, I first focus on the substantive outcomes of my study and then move to the quantitative examination. I will first set up the operationalization of my research and then move on to the analysis.

DEPENDENT VARIABLES

Until recently, data that specifically measures property transaction costs has been limited, and thus, scholars have used proxies such as exchange rates, the rule of law, and credit markets as surrogate measures (Leblang 1996). I have identified three categories of property transaction cost measures that I deem to be most appropriate and most direct measures from the World Bank Doing Business Economic Database (2013) which include: 1) *registration of property*, 2) *enforcement of contracts*, and 3) *access to credit*. As shown in Table 3.1, each of the three categories consists of separate measures of property transaction costs. The three categories of measures help examine the three dimensions in the property costs debate: 1) NAS law tenure's association with registration and land transferring, 2) NAS law tenure's association with the enforcement of contracts, and 3) NAS law association with capital garnered through credit access. Next, I discuss the operationalization of the three measures by the World Bank Doing Business Economic data (2013).

Table 3.1. Dependent Property Transaction Cost Variables

Category	*Measures*		
Registration of Property	Procedures required for businesses to secure a property	Time in calendar days needed to secure a property	The cost recorded as a percentage of the property value
Enforcement of Contracts	Procedural steps of a commercial dispute	Time in calendar days from the filing of the lawsuit in court	Cost recorded as a percentage of the claim
Access to Credit	The private credit bureau coverage	The public credit registry coverage	

Because of the exploratory nature of my dependent variable, I consider each of the three categories separately because each substantively captures a different dimension of property transaction costs. I estimate eight individual OLS models, one for each of the eight measures. The measures of property transaction costs have different metrics; thus, I chose not to create a composite score. For example, a measure may have time in days for a transaction to take place, the costs making the transaction, and the number of procedural steps in the transaction which are all different and thus cannot be combined. Furthermore, when I employ the Cronbach Alpha test, I find no internal consistency among the variables, showing that composite scores have no reliability.[4] Therefore, I create eight OLS models displayed in Tables 3.3 through 3.5, representing the registration of property, enforcement of contracts, and access to credit.

The World Bank Doing Business Economic Database (2013), operationalizes the registration of property, enforcement of contracts, and access to credit in the following manner:

Registration of Property: I use three measures depicting the registration of property: 1) the number of procedures required for businesses to secure a property. 2) the time in calendar days needed for businesses to secure a property, and 3) the costs recorded as a percentage of the property value, assumed equivalent to 50 times income per capita (only official costs required by law are recorded).

Enforcement of Contracts: I use three measures depicting the enforcement of contracts: 1) the list of procedural steps compiled for each economy traces the chronology of a commercial dispute before the relevant court. 2) costs recorded as a percentage of the claim, assumed to be equivalent to 200% of income per capita (no bribes are recorded, and three types of court costs, enforcement costs and average attorney fees, and 3) the time required in calendar days from the filing of the lawsuit in court until the final determination.

Access to Credit: I use two measures depicting access to credit: 1) the private credit bureau coverage that reports the number of individuals or firms listed by a private credit bureau with current information on repayment history, unpaid debts, or credit outstanding as percentage of adults. 2) the public credit registry coverage reporting the number of individuals and firms listed in a public credit registry with current information on repayment history, unpaid debts, or credit outstanding as percentage of adults.

INDEPENDENT VARIABLES

NAS Law (Protection): As I have noted, I examine the effect of NAS law on property transaction costs. As shown in chapter 1, I have created an original data set for neo-autogenous law provisions, years 1952–2013. In addition, I created an additive index protection which examines the level of protection for NAS law in state constitutions (combines constitutional protection and Protection of Institutions). Substantively, my two measures—formal recognition of NAS law and recognition of specific institutions—represent a category of constitutional treatment of NAS law described in chapter two. I conducted a factor analysis to identify the underlying structure of my two measures of national tolerance for NAS law. The analysis clearly demonstrated one factor or dimension. The factor, which I term "protection" includes the recognition measure, which has the strongest association with a correlation of 0.8458 and the institution's measure, which has the second strongest correlation with a correlation of 0.8315. The two variables capture the level of constitutional protection provided through legal recognition of customary law generally and its institutions more specifically. To investigate these patterns further statistically, I created an additive index protection (combines constitutional protection and protection of institutions) as reported in Table 3.2. Protection of NAS law is my key independent variable—a six-point scale, ranging from –1 to 4 with a reliability of 0.89.

Table 3.2. Protection Descriptive

Variable	*N*	*Mean*	*Std. Dev.*	*Min*	*Max*	*Category*	*Freq.*	*Per (%)*
Protection	1008	1.16	1.60	–1	4	4	180	17.9
						3	46	4.6
						2	126	12.5
						1	106	10.5
						0	505	50.1
						–1	45	4.5

Category Description:
4 - very high-level protection
3 - high-level protection
2 - medium-level protection
1 - low-level protection
0 - no protection
–1 - intolerance/banning

Democracy: Desoto (2000) and Leblang (1996) both argue that an efficient political establishment lowers property transaction costs. Furthermore, Leblang and North (1992) both assert that democratic states have lower property transaction costs because of checks on institutions. For *level of democracy*, I use data from the Polity IV data set. The Polity IV data set conceives of democracy as "1) the presence of institutions and procedures through which citizens can express effective preferences about alternative policies and leaders, 2) the existence of institutionalized constraints on the exercise of power by the executive, and 3) the guarantee of civil liberties to all citizens in their daily lives and in acts of political participation" (Polity IV). The democracy indicator has an additive eleven-point scale (0-10). The operational indicator of democracy derives from coding of the competitiveness of political participation (variable 2.6), the openness and competitiveness of executive recruitment (variables 2.3 and 2.2), and constraints on the chief executive (Polity IV).

State Context Variables: I employ five variables that depict state context. Ault and Rutman (1979) assert that as long as transaction costs were positive the Africans had little incentive to exercise individual ownership when supply exceeded demand. However, the individual exercised ownership to property once the demand for resources exceeded supply at zero price. The conditions within the state may increase scarcity, leading to higher transaction costs. I employ five measures that capture state context. The five measures include: 1) the *geographical size* of the state capturing the amount of available land (by author), 2) the *population size* and 3) the *population growth* capturing the increasing population pressure with number of persons competing for property (World Bank data). In addition, I employ 4) *per capita GDP* capturing a state's economic capacity (constant 2000 $) (World Bank data), and 5) *urbanization* which captures a percentage of the population living in urban areas, which reduces dependency on land mostly in the rural areas governed under NAS law (World Bank data).

Substantive Findings and Analysis

As stated earlier, I first make a substantive summary of the major findings in consideration of the larger audience. Overall, my analyses demonstrate strong support for the communalist perspective and only minor support for the individualist perspective. I present a summary assessment across all arguments—registration of property, enforcement of contracts and access to credit in Table 3.3.

When examining the Table, "+" means that NAS law led to an increase in property transaction costs in the particular category, "-" means that NAS law led to a decrease in property transaction costs, and "0" means the presence of NAS law had no effect on property transaction costs in the particular category. Three of the "–" arguments support the communalist perspective, two "+" arguments support the individualist perspective, and three "–" insignifi-

Table 3.3. Analyzed Property Transaction Cost Arguments

Component	*Measures*	*Protection of NAS Law*	*Perspective Supported*
Registration of Property	Number of Procedures	0	Communalist
	Time Required	0	Communalist
	Property Value Costs	–	Communalist
Enforcing of Contracts	Number of Procedures	–	Communalist
	Time Required	0	Communalist
	Enforcement Costs	+	Individualist
Access to Credit	Public Coverage	–	Communalist
	Private Coverage	+	Individualist

"+" Increased transaction costs (Individualists) (count 2)
"–" Decreased transaction costs (communalists) (count 3)
"0" No effect on transaction costs (communalists) (count 3)

cant arguments support the communalist perspective. To be specific, of the eight potential arguments, less than a third support the individualist perspective while over two-thirds support the communalist perspective. In addition, the analysis supports one of the key assertions by communalists that empirical evidence does not support neo-economic claims for the primary expected benefit, reduced property transaction costs, by moving to one state-led statutory law tenure system. Communalists' arguments appear to be more accurate and substantive than those of the individualists from my empirical analysis.

EMPIRICAL FINDINGS AND ANALYSIS

To test my hypothesis, I estimate eight OLS models reported in Tables 3.4 through 3.6. In addition, I check my results by estimating eight parallel fixed effects (FE) models. Furthermore, since I am running OLS regressions, the reported coefficient from the independent variables show the size of effect and direction of effect, except on the logged variables. In Table 3.4, the three

Table 3.4. Registration of Property

	Procedures		*Time*		*Costs*	
Variable	*RE*	*FE*	*RE*	*FE*	*RE*	*FE*
Protection (+/–)	0.13	0.13	–2.99	–3.02	**–9.47**	**–9.44**
	(0.08)	(0.08)	(2.87)	(2.83)	(2.66)	(2.63)
Level Democracy (–)	**–0.13**	**–0.13**	–1.17	–1.18	0.16	0.03
	(0.04)	(0.04)	(1.25)	(1.23)	(1.17)	(1.16)
Log GDP Per Capita (–)	**0.33**	**0.35**	–5.94	–2.09	1.96	3.91
	(0.13)	(0.13)	(4.41)	(4.44)	(4.18)	(4.19)
Log Geographical Size of the State in Thousands (–)	**–0.36**	**–0.37**	**–18.86**	**–20.25**	**6.84**	**5.83**
	(0.08)	(0.09)	(2.89)	(2.87)	(2.69)	(2.68)
Log Population Total (+)	**0.72**	**0.73**	**9.98**	**11.78**	**–7.97**	–7.01
	(0.12)	(0.12)	(4.12)	(4.07)	(3.88)	(3.87)
Population Growth (+)	**0.44**	**0.45**	9.79	**11.64**	5.73	6.71
	(0.17)	(0.17)	(5.72)	(5.65)	(5.35)	(5.32)
Urban Population (–)	**–0.02**	**–0.02**	0.22	0.23	**–0.54**	**–0.52**
	(0.01)	(0.01)	(0.27)	(0.27)	(0.25)	(0.25)
Constant	**–4.84**	**–5.24**	43.65	–8.83	**193.99**	**168.11**
	(2.00)	(2.05)	(68.56)	(68.58)	(65.35)	(65.27)
N	357	357	357	357	335	335
R-Sq	0.2	0.37	0.2	0.2	0.08	0.07

Bolded coefficients are significant at $p < 0.05$
(Standard Errors)

Table 3.5. Enforcing of Contracts

	Procedures		*Time*		*Costs*	
Variable	*RE*	*FE*	*RE*	*FE*	*RE*	*FE*
Protection (+/–)	**–1.06**	–1.06	6.11	6.05	**104.20**	**104.65**
	(0.20)	(0.20)	(11.09)	(11.20)	(14.69)	(14.83)
Level Democracy (–)	–0.08	–0.08	**17.46**	**17.57**	7.52	7.62
	(0.09)	(0.09)	(4.84)	(4.89)	(6.33)	(6.39)
Log GDP per capita (–)	**–0.73**	**–0.71**	10.45	12.29	**–101.80**	**–108.52**
	(0.31)	(0.32)	(17.01)	(17.58)	(22.32)	(23.12)
Log Geographical Size of the State in Thousands (–)	**0.55**	**0.55**	12.59	12.04	**–34.23**	**–32.05**
	(0.20)	(0.21)	(11.15)	(11.35)	(14.61)	(14.84)
Log Population Total (+)	–0.22	–0.21	**–61.92**	**–60.68**	12.87	10.26
	(0.29)	(0.29)	(15.88)	(16.13)	(20.78)	(21.08)
Population Growth (+)	0.41	0.42	**57.47**	**58.35**	**88.75**	**85.78**
	(0.40)	(0.41)	(22.07)	(22.38)	(28.85)	(29.23)
Urban Population (–)	–0.01	–0.01	–0.14	–0.14	**5.88**	**5.89**
	(0.02)	(0.02)	(1.05)	(1.06)	(1.39)	(1.40)
Constant	**45.83**	**45.66**	**1273.79**	**1241.83**	436.29	517.44
	(4.80)	(4.93)	(264.42)	(271.51)	(345.66)	(354.71)
N	358	358	357	357	349	349
R-Sq	0.22	0.2	0.1	0.1	0.2	0.2

Bolded coefficients are significant at $p < 0.05$
(Standard Errors)

dependent variables represent the *registration of property*, in Table 3.5 the three dependent variables depict *the enforcement of contracts*, and in Table 3.6 the two dependent variables represent *access to credit*. Despite demonstrating validity for some arguments posited by each perspective, my analysis overwhelmingly supports the communalist arguments.

I first examine the key independent variable protection of NAS law which produces mixed results. Regarding the registration of property in Table 3.4, the protection for NAS law does not affect two of the measures: the number of procedures and the time required, which in part supports the communalist hypothesis that NAS law does not affect registration costs. Furthermore, protection decreases registration of property costs: a one-unit increase change protection reduces registration costs by 474 dollars, equivalent to a year's worth of daily wages for 46.8% of the sub-Saharan population living on 1.25 dollars a day.[5] Once again we see mixed results in regard to the enforcement of contracts in Table 3.5. Protection produces mixed results as an increase in protection decreases procedures while it increases costs. More specifically, a one-unit increase in protection reduces the number of enforcement procedures by 1.06 procedures, while the same change would increase the enforce-

Table 3.6. Access to Credit

	Public Coverage		*Private Coverage*	
Variable	*RE*	*FE*	*RE*	*FE*
Protection (+/–)	**–16.74**	**–16.73**	**16.99**	**16.89**
	(2.32)	(2.33)	(4.60)	(4.64)
Level of Democracy (+)	**4.19**	**4.18**	3.61	3.58
	(1.02)	(1.02)	(2.02)	(2.04)
Log GDP Per Capita (+)	**17.30**	**15.82**	**56.07**	**56.46**
	(3.59)	(3.72)	(7.17)	(7.42)
Log Geographical Size of the State in Thousands (+)	**–12.45**	**–11.79**	**30.87**	**30.64**
	(2.35)	(2.39)	(4.62)	(4.71)
Log Population Total (–)	5.73	5.05	**–28.86**	**–28.78**
	(3.32)	(3.35)	(6.66)	(6.75)
Population Growth (–)	**–11.90**	**–12.67**	**–31.95**	**–31.93**
	(4.64)	(4.68)	(9.24)	(9.36)
Urban Population (+)	0.26	0.27	**–2.00**	**–1.99**
	(0.22)	(0.22)	(0.44)	(0.44)
Constant	–91.04	–71.85	76.32	73.83
	(55.42)	(56.67)	(111.99)	(114.43)
N	345	345	345	345
R-Sq	0.34	0.4	0.5	0.5

Bolded coefficients are significant at $p < 0.05$
(Standard Errors)

ment costs by 209 dollars or half a year's worth of daily income. The decrease in procedures may be due to familiarity with NAS tenure law; however, the high enforcement costs may be due to ambiguity as they pertain to ownership, making it costly to enforce contracts as asserted by Joireman (2007). Moreover, regarding access to credit in Table 3.6, protection of NAS law also produces mixed results, with an increase in protection decreasing credit as reported by the public bureau, but increasing access to credit as reported by the private bureau. The analyses show that a one-unit increase in protection decreases access to credit to 17 individuals or firms as reported by the public credit bureau. In contrast, a one-unit change in protection increases access to credit to 17 individuals or firms according to the private credit bureau report.

Next, I address the other variables in the models. First, in contrast to expectation, democracy produces mixed results. A one-unit increase in the level of democracy decreases the number of procedures to register property by 0.0013 procedures and increases by level of access to credit to 4 individuals or firms as reported by the public credit bureau; however, democracy increases the time of enforcement of contracts by almost three weeks. Furthermore, GDP per capita, in contrast to expectation, also produces mixed results. A 1 percent increase in logged GDP per capita increases registration procedures by

0.0033 procedures, and decreases enforcement of contract procedures and costs by 0.0073 procedures and 2.04 dollars. In addition, a 1 percent increase in logged GDP per capita increases access to credit to 1 individual or firm as reported by both the public and private credit bureaus. Furthermore, state geographical size produces mixed results. A 1 percent increase in logged state geographical size decreases the registration of property procedures and time by 0.0036 procedures and a day. In addition, a 1 percent increase in logged state size increases enforcement of contract procedures by 0.0055 procedures, while reducing enforcement costs 2.04 dollars. Moreover, a 1 percent increase in logged state geographical size decreases credit coverage to 1 person or firm as reported by both the public credit bureau and the private credit bureau. Furthermore, in contrast to expectation, population total produces mixed results. A percent increase in logged population total increases registration of property procedures and time by 0.0072 procedures and a day, while reducing registration costs by 399[6] dollars, a significant reduction of about a year's worth of daily wages. Moreover, in regard to the enforcement of contracts, a 1 percent increase in logged population total decreases enforcement time by a day, while the same increase decreases access to credit to 1 individual or firm as reported by a private credit bureau.

Turning to population growth, the effect of population growth appears to be particularly important as it performs consistently across all models, increasing property transaction costs. My analysis supports the assertion by Ault and Rutman (1979) that ultimately the problem of property transaction costs lays in understanding the economics of property as scarcity in property and increasing population pressures create the main shift in the evolution of property law. Furthermore, according to the UN World Prospects 2015, between 2015 and 2050 more than half of the global population growth will occur in Africa.[7] The UN adds that Africa has the highest pace of growth estimated to be 2.55% annually.[8] The implications of sub-Sahara's high population growth will be increased scarcity in property, particularly land, high property transactions costs, and ultimately reduced economic gains and conflict over resources. More specifically, a 1 percent increase in population growth increases the number of registration of property procedures by 0.44 procedures and time by 2 weeks, and the enforcement of contracts time by over 2 months, and costs by 178 dollars. In addition, a one percent increase in population growth decreases access to credit to 12 people or firms as reported by the public credit bureau and to 32 individuals or firms as reported by the private credit bureau. Finally, in contrast to expectations, urbanization produces mixed results. A 1 percent increase in the urban population decreases registration of property procedures by 0.02 procedures and registration costs by 27 dollars, while increasing the costs of enforcing contracts by 11.76

dollars. Lastly, a 1 percent increase in urbanization decreases the number of people with access to credit by 2 individuals or firms as reported by a private credit bureau.

Overall, the findings in Tables 3.4 through 3.6, demonstrate consistency with the protection models; all the recognition models' and all, but one, of the institution models' coefficients retain the same directions and have a stronger impact. The robust test models support my analysis that a majority of the findings support the communalist perspective over the individualist perspective.

CONCLUSION

The greater contribution of the study is that it is not just a normative debate or empirical analysis, but the examination of a significant policy area that affects 46.8 percent or 455 million sub-Saharans who live on 1.25 dollars a day, most of whom are agrarian and depend on land for their livelihood. Reduction in property transactions costs can help people move a significant number of people out of poverty. There are several substantive contributions that the chapter has brought to African studies. First, I make a normative analysis of two differing perspectives on how to handle property. With a significantly large agrarian population, sub-Saharan states cannot ignore the importance of making good policies when it comes to property tenure. The individualist perspective argued for a state-led tenure system, while communalists argued for a pluralist tenure system that included NAS law tenure. In order to analyze both arguments empirically, I performed an exploratory multidisciplinary quantitative examination that combines political and legal arguments with those of business and economic disciplines to produce several insights on the most efficient and most equitable property tenure system. I make a contribution to the study of NAS law by challenging the assumption of exclusive accuracy from any of the perspectives; however, I am able to conclude that the communalist arguments have a high level of empirical accuracy with the majority of the evidence supporting the communalist perspective. The finding is significant because it supports the need to further assess the importance of NAS law tenure. My study suggests caution on the push toward a state-led statutory tenure law system. Chimhowu and Woodhouse (2006) assert, "[The] position underlying many African government plans for tenure reform, usually advocates some form of adjudication to convert customary rights to state-recognized property rights (347)." In conclusion, my analysis suggests that NAS law tenure can add value to sub-Saharan states and benefits those who cannot afford the likely financial impact of a transition to a state-led statutory law system.

NOTES

1. Land tenure refers the legal system holding the land (whether NAS law or Statutory law).

2. As explained in chapter 2, I continue to term customary law as neo-autogenous law (NAS law) because a majority emerged from the indigenous sub-Saharan population and was revived or modified by external influences (mostly from colonial experience).

3. First clearance rights pertain to a clan or ethnic group who claim to be the first (according to their knowledge) to clear a ground/piece of land not inhibited by anyone prior to their arrival, normally occurring when first settlers turn old-growth/virgin forests in homesteads or farms.

4. Furthermore, I do factor analysis and find that all variables have high levels of uniqueness.

5. World Bank Data: Topic Poverty, Accessed: 10-5-15, http://data.worldbank.org/topic/poverty.

6. Significant only in the random effects model.

7. United Nations, Department of Economic and Social Affairs, Population Division (2015). World Population Prospects: The 2015 Revision, Key Findings and Advance Tables. Working Paper No. ESA/P/WP.241. http://esa.un.org/unpd/wpp/Publications/Files/Key_Findings_WPP_2015.pdf.

8. Ibid.

Chapter Four

NAS Law and Women's Rights Attainment

Women's political, social, and economic rights attainment remains an important topic with strong policy implications, especially in light of reports of continuing gaps.[1] The UN millennium development goals include women's attainment and equality as one of the eight key areas of development. Furthermore, the UN reported in the Millennium Development Goals Report 2015 of persistent gaps in women's attainment despite major improvements.[2] I examine two differing perspectives on the women's rights debate—the critical and positive perspectives. Critics of the persistent gaps in women's attainment point to NAS law as a key contributing factor that impedes women's attainment because of its communal and conservative nature (Hyde 2013; Ashena 2003; Joireman 2007; Grant 2006; Tripp 2004; An-Na'im 2003; Ashena 2003; Mondlane 2003). The critical perspective posits that the proper progress in women's attainment requires removal of NAS law in exchange for civil or common law. On the other hand, the positive perspective asserts that empirically NAS law does not impede women's attainment, and to have a better understanding of gender relations in sub-Saharan African, analysis should be during examining the pre-colonial period, then the colonial and post-colonial, to the present in order to have a greater appreciation of the context. Scholars caution against a simplistic view of NAS law and argue for a more in-depth examination of the history between NAS law and its interaction with women's rights attainment to create proper policies that improve human dignity and equity.

In addition, in the chapter I examine two case studies that are presented to test the two perspectives empirically. Specifically, I analyze the South African Supreme Court cases of Bhe and Shibi, two women who challenged decisions made under NAS law concerning their inheritance and protection (Grant 2006). After that I engage in a rigorous empirical research analysis examining the effect of national tolerance for neo-autogenous law on women's attainment. Overall, my findings produce a more nuanced understanding of how NAS law interacts with different aspects of women's rights attainment.

THE CRITICAL PERSPECTIVE

I term the first perspective the critical perspective, which argues that NAS law impedes women's attainment. The literature points to the reinterpretation of NAS law during colonization in favor of men and to the patrimonial nature of NAS law as the causes for NAS law's negative relation to women's attainment. The negative view argues that, as part of a dual legal system, NAS law can erode formal protections for youth and women. Richards and Haglund (2015) claim that in Botswana, the protections against marital rape exist only for marriages through the formal legal systems, but a majority of persons choose to get married in the traditional system, negating any protections law would have to offer. They further assert that such dual systems can drastically interfere with the ability of women to "engage the state." The critical perspective also asserts that the colonialists implemented systems that improved women's rights. As Hyden (2013) argues, women have rights under common or civil law systems as established by the colonial powers, but only a small percentage of women can claim the rights due to NAS law (171). He adds that women have fewer rights, if any, under NAS law as interpreted today. However, he, in contrast, also states that, "Judges in colonial days did little to challenge the existing patriarchal tradition, and with social change brought about by capitalism and urbanization, the conditions of women often deteriorated" (171). Shadle (2003) asserts that when Europeans turned over judicial work to senior African elders and chiefs, they adjudicated NAS law and made interpretations that expanded their powers, and repressed women and youth. Concomitantly, the reinterpretation of NAS law during the colonial era caused women's issues to have no voice in the political process and diminished the opportunity of women to improve their social standing. In addition, critics of NAS law assert that the patrimonial nature of NAS law hinders women's attainment. Hyden (2006)'s uses the social exchange theory to argue that the manifestation of power in different degrees of social dependence leaves men having superior power under NAS law. Subsequently, the power dynamics cause men to have rights over property, women, and juniors. Overall, the critical perspective argues for the need to exchange NAS law for colonial inherited systems of common and civil law to increase women's rights attainment. The critical perspective then would argue that increasing constitutional provisions that protect NAS law would negatively affect women's attainment.

Critical Perspective Hypothesis: Higher levels of constitutional protections for NAS law will have a negative effect on women's rights attainment.

THE POSITIVE PERSPECTIVE

Next, I turn to the second perspective that I term the positive perspective that supports NAS law and argues for the legal viability of the law, arguing that it has actually played a role in women's attainment. These scholars do not argue against the continuous evolution and examination of NAS law like any other type of law, but rather they argue that legal reforms should take into consideration NAS law and not assume it to be an inferior law (Fallon 2008; An-Na'm 2003; Chimhowu and Woodhouse 2006; Bennett 1990; Ault and Rutman 1979). These scholars assert that most of the criticisms of NAS law lack factual evidence and thus require empirical examination. The positive perspective argues that the main problem with the critical perspective comes from the misunderstanding of history as it pertains to the neo-autogenous law and institutions, and the colonial regime. Scholars fault the critical perspective's misrepresentation of the role that colonial inherited systems played in women's attainment. Fallon (2008) asserts that the colonialist system was not equitable, but rather was male-centric and suppressed women's attainment. She adds that under the colonial inherited systems, women did not have the same structural opportunities because colonial systems provided fewer structural opportunities for women to participate in the colonial state. In a similar manner, Ilumoka (1994) asserts that colonial education and employment policies differentiated public (the colonial system) and the private (the neo-autogenous system) by providing sub-Saharan men access to the "public sphere" while denying women access (317). Colonialists favored male political and economic attainment over that of women. The colonialists selected African male leaders from autogenous systems to participate in the colonial system, while denying female neo-autogenous leaders the same opportunities in education or in political posts, which reflected the White male-centric European model. Fallon (2008) asserts that historically in sub-Saharan Africa, neo-autogenous systems provided women with social and political structural opportunities for participation within the neo-autogenous institutions (3-5). As stated ealier, "Under many pre-colonial systems of social organizations, sexual divisions of labor did not necessarily imply patriarchal oppression. . . . The work of both sexes and all groups was valued as necessary to the function of the society, and women's reproductive roles were sometimes given great premium" (llumka 1994, 317). For example, the Igbo of Nigeria had a female representative selected as the mother of the community, who worked with a female cabinet to address women's concerns.[3] In addition, in Kenya prior to colonization, the Kikuyu had a system where after initiation men and women enjoyed equality in membership in the society. Furthermore, with the Yoruba, women contributed to the political structures by holding different political offices with various levels of rank and responsibility which included participating in the selection of the King, running the treasury, and running the capital city.[4] Other examples abound: in South Africa a female monarch leads the Lovedu people, in Sierra Leone 10 out of 81 paramount chiefs were women, and in Ghana, queen mothers still exist and yield much political influence.[5]

However, according to the positive argument, colonial-inherited systems subordinated neo-autogenous systems to the colonial-inherited systems. Thus, despite the high levels of empowerment in neo-autogenous systems, women held relatively less power than their male counterparts in the colonial state, and over time the state was viewed as the domain of men and provided limited entry to women (Fallon 2008; Bennett 1991). After independence, many regimes engaged in authoritarian rule, maintaining some of the male-centric colonial structures. The centralization of state power limited any form of resistance, including women's movements. Fallon asserts that after independence, authoritarian regimes coopted women's groups into large state-run organizations in order to reduce their opposition against authoritative regimes; however, women remained organized in NAS systems and community organizations.

Improvements in women's attainment at the state level occurred as states democratized in the late 1980s to the 1990s because of democratic opportunities structures opening up and enabling women to engage the state. Refining Fallon (2008) arguments further, we can predict that NAS law can provide a level of political attainment that deviates from the predominant and critical view of NAS law deterring women's rights attainment as democratization increases. While women had little to no participation in colonial systems, they continued to participate and remained organized in neo-autogenous systems that provided opportunity structures for their participation and organization. Women effectively engaged the state because they were organized and had prior experience with power under neo-autogenous systems (3). Fallon asserts that because of NAS institutions, community organizations, and structural opportunities brought about by democratization, women's legislative representation increased from 0.94 percent at independence to 7.78 percent in the 1990s with democratization, and up to 17.4 percent by 2008 (37). According to UN Women, female parliamentary representation in Africa has risen to 23 percent, currently above the global average of 22 percent.[6] One must then question, how can a region of the world that is usually condemned as anti-women's right attainment, have not only the fastest growing, but also among the highest levels of attainment for women as compared to other states globally. More significantly, sub-Saharan Africa represents almost half of the top ten states with the highest levels of representation globally, with Rwanda having the highest level of political participation in the world at 63.80 percent.[7] Furthermore, examples of women in leadership include, women as prime ministers in Mozambique, Sao Tome, Senegal, Guinea Bissau, Mali, Madagascar, and, Malawi. As well, women have served as nationally elected heads of states—Malawi President Joyce Bandaa, Liberian President Ellen Jonson-Sirleaf, and Mauritius President Ameenah Gurib, and women as house speakers in Ethiopia, Lesotho and South Africa, and deputy speakers in Uganda and Zimbabwe. Overall, the positive perspective argues that NAS law would have a positive effect on women's attainment with increased democratization. The constitutional promulgation of NAS law provisions, in part, depicts the preference of a significant majority of sub-Saharans willing to maintain their indigenous systems that provided opportunity structures for women. I argue that the positive perspective would predict that provisions that protect NAS law in state constitutions do not negatively affect women's attainment.

In conclusion, the major question between the two perspectives is whether NAS law has a place in modern Africa or whether it should be replaced with other legal forms. It is interesting to note that both perspectives, in part, point to the effect of colonial policies. In addition, with the destruction of original ethnic societal government structures in certain colonies, taking of communal land by White settlers, forced and volunteered movement of the population to the cities, and titling of property to heads of the family may also have played a part in disenfranchising sub-Saharans.

Positive Perspective Hypothesis: Higher levels of constitutional protections for NAS law will have a neutral or positive effect on women's attainment.

Next, I examine two case studies to test the two perspectives empirically. I analyze the Bhe and Shibi cases that came before the South African Supreme Court to examine the interaction between NAS law decisions and women's rights attainment. The cases are unique in that they examine both legislative policies and judicial decisions in South Africa, and their effect on NAS law and women's attainment.

THE BHE AND SHIBI CASE STUDIES

In the Bhe and Shibi cases (*Bhe and Others v Magistrate, Khayelitsha and Others*; *Shibi v Sithole and Others*) the Supreme Court of South Africa had to rule on the merits of the Intestate Succession Act of 1987 that differentiated African inheritance from that of the Afrikaners, and the Black Administration Act that provided for inheritance through African male primogeniture. The cases were heard together under the direction of the Chief Justice. The first case was that of Ms. Bhe and her two daughters whom she had out of wedlock with her lover who had passed on. Bhe had been forcibly removed from the land by the father of her deceased lover whom she had lived with for 12 years. In turn, Ms. Bhe filed an application to Cape High Court challenging the father's claim of inheritance, since he claimed male primogeniture. Turning to the Shibi case, all of Shibi's immediate male relatives were deceased and the property of her husband was given to a male cousin who removed Shibi from the land. In addition to the two court filings, there were cases filed by the Women's Legal Center Trust, an organized interest, and the South African Human Rights Commission, a governmental advocacy institution questioning the unconstitutionality of the whole of section 23 of the Black Act which they found to be inconsistent with the rights to equality and human dignity. After listening to the cases, the South African Supreme Court ruled in favor of the plaintiffs, arguing the Intestate Succession Act of 1987 was created on the basis of race, separating white and black, and not gender, therefore the application of NAS law in those cases did not apply, since the act was discriminatory and against human dignity. Furthermore, they found that section 23 of the Black Act was racist and unconstitutional. On the rulings, the positive perspective could be argued to have been supported by the judicial decision. However, Grant (2006) brings in a caveat by asserting that the Court was empowered under section 172 of the Constitution to make any order on NAS law succession. In other words, the Court could rule for female inheritance but they deferred the matter to the legislature. The principle that the Court used to rule was actually the merits of the right to maintenance which is a NAS law principle. The principle of the right of maintenance asserts that the family unit, which includes women, their children, and youth, have a right to be preserved and protected by the holder of the communal land. It was on this principle that the Court found in both cases the plaintiffs had been neglected by the holders of the land, the male heirs. The Court did not venture to change any of the succession rules under NAS law, arguing that the parliament has the responsibility to create laws that pertain to NAS law inheritance, and not the Courts. The dissenting opinion agreed with the ruling but argued that NAS law should evolve toward current times and the courts should help with such evolution. While racial discriminatory policies were ruled unconstitutional, the Court did not rule against promigratory or male inheritance practiced by certain ethnic nations, but on the misuse and misinterpretation of NAS law. Such a ruling speaks to the reality that NAS law continues to be a major part of the sub-Saharan legal and social experience. Therefore, the ruling by the Court actually supports the positive perspective when examining actual NAS law principles and not the skewed application of NAS law. The case study also helps demonstrate that colonial policies that were male centric permeated into the application of NAS law which continued into post-independent Africa. The Bhe and Shibi cases demonstrate the need for legislative bodies to engage in making the legal type more equitable to all people to live under NAS law.

TESTING NAS LAW'S RELATION TO WOMEN'S ATTAINMENT

As I have noted above, I engage in an empirical research analysis, examining the effect of national tolerance for neo-autogenous law on women's attainment. My unit of analysis is county-year. The data cover all 49 sub-Saharan states. I estimate OLS models with continuous dependent variables. As with the previous chapter, due to my split audience, those with quantitative backgrounds and without, I first focus on the substantive outcomes of my study and then move to the quantitative examination. I will first set up the operationalization of my research and then move on to the analysis.

DEPENDENT VARIABLE–POLITICAL RIGHTS ATTAINMENT

I operationalize political attainment as the ability of women to access a decision-making body. As stated above, I employ a specific indicator of political attainment and World Bank data on the *proportion of seats held by women in national parliaments*, as a percentage of parliamentary seats in a singling or lower house for years 1997–2013. Table 4.1 displays the descriptive statistics for dependent variables of political rights attainment. On the issue of endogeneity, whether a correlation between NAS law and women's attainment measures exists, I argue that we would expect that NAS law would affect women's attainment and not women's attainment affecting NAS law. I argue that constitutional protections for NAS law occurred decades before the increase in women's attainment in the 1980s and 1990s (Fallon 2008; Paxton et al. 2010; Hyden 2013). As Fallon (2008) argues, women's legislative representation increased from 0.94 percent at independence to 7.78 percent in the 1990s, and to 17.4 percent by 2008 (37). Likewise, Paxton and partners (2010) assert, "Women made up only 2 per cent of world parliamentarians in 1945, 5 per cent in 1970 and 9 per cent in 1990 . . . [in] 2000, women

Table 4.1. Descriptive Statistics for Dependent Variables Political Rights Attainment

Variable	*N*	*Mean*	*Std. Dev.*	*Min*	*Max*	*Years*
World Bank–Share of Legislative Seats	752	14.79	10.21	0	63.8	1997–2013

still had barely surpassed 10 per cent of parliamentary seats (11.7 per cent)" (27). From my analysis, I find that that the two measures of protection—recognition of NAS law and protection for specific NAS law institutions—had a positive mean from the onset of independence. In fact, in the decade of the 1960s, recognition has a mean of 0.7, and institution has a mean of 0.54, out of a possible 1. Therefore, I assert, we should not find endogeneity problems with the study.

CONTROL VARIABLES

I examine thirteen control variables in the political attainment model. I control for the level of democratization using Polity IV data and do checks on my analysis using Davenport and Armstrong's (2004) categorization, where they scale the Polity IV 11-point scale into a trichotomous measure. I also control for world society influences (CEDAW, ICESCR, CEDAW optional protocol and ICESCR optional protocol). Furthermore, I include three domestic quota types (reserved seats quotas, legal candidate quotas, and political quotas). I also include state capacity (GDP per capita, geographic size, population total, population growth).

Democracy: Several studies posit that democracy improves human rights practices (Keith 1999; Hafner-Burton and Tsutsui 2005; Neumayer 2005; Englehart and Miller 2014). Likewise, Fallon (2008) argues that democratization helps improve women's political attainment because of political opportunity structures that allow women to engage the state. Landman (2005) adds that newer democracies, of which the majority of sub-Saharan states are, will have higher levels of political attainment. I employ the *level of democracy* data from the Polity IV data set. The Polity IV data set defines democracy as "1) the presence of institutions and procedures through which citizens can express effective preferences about alternative policies and leaders, 2) the existence of institutionalized constraints on the exercise of power by the executive, and 3) the guarantee of civil liberties to all citizens in their daily lives and in acts of political participation" (Polity IV). The democracy indicator is an additive eleven-point scale (0-10) derived from coding of the competitiveness of political participation, the openness and competitiveness of executive recruitment, and constraints on the chief executive (Polity IV). In addition, I recreate Davenport and Armstrong's (2004) categorization of the Polity IV trichotomous measure with "1" depicting low levels of democracy (0-7), "2" depicting a medium level of democracy (8-9) and "3" depicting high levels of democracy (10).

Interaction Varible—Democracy and NAS Law: Fallon (2008) asserts that NAS law systems and community organization kept women organized while they were marginalized from the colonial-based modern state governing systems. When democratization increased, women who were already experienced in NAS law and in community systems took advantage of the new opportunity structures and were able to enter state politics. Therefore, the interaction between democracy and NAS law should have a positive impact on women's political attainment.

World Society: According to the world society perspective, as states participate and interact in the world society, they converge toward globally accepted standards, identities, and norms. More specifically, the world society influences states through their level of participation in the global civil society and level of membership in international governmental organizations (Boli and Thomas 1997; Go 2003). I examine two international women's covenants; the *CEDAW* and the *ICESCR*. In order to code my data on CEDAW and ICESCR, I obtained information from the United Nations Office of the High Commissioner for Human Rights. For the CEDAW, I code the individual country level adoption to the CEDAW, which is appropriate here because it deals primarily with first generation civil and political rights. I code the CEDAW as (2-ratified, 1-signed, 0-not signed or ratified). For the ICESCR, I code the individual country level adoption to the ICESCR, which is appropriate here because it deals primarily with second generation social and cultural rights. I code the ICESCR as (2-ratified, 1-signed, 0-not signed or ratified. I also test whether ratifying the optional protocols depict higher levels of commitment to international treaties, and I code states that have signed the *CEDAW optional protocol* and the *ICESCR optional protocol* as (2-ratified, 1-signed, 0-not signed or ratified).

Gender Quotas: I include political quotas that affect the level of women's political attainment. Paxton, Hughes, and Painter II (2010) argue that quotas positively affect women's representation. I code data on quota from information provided in the gender quota project and state governments' legal documents.[8] I coded three types of quotas: 1) *reserved seat quota* (reserved seats regulate the number of women elected), 2) *legal candidate quota* (a minimum for the share of women on the candidate lists as a legal requirement) and 3) *voluntary party quota* (a minimum for the share of women on the candidate lists as a measure written into the statutes of individual political parties). All the data was coded "1" if a state was in the category, and "0" if not.

State Capacity Variables: One of the reasons why sub-Saharan states may have low levels of women's attainment may be due to the state capacity. Sub-Saharan states have had independence for roughly 50 years and most of the states are still developing their political, economic, legal, and security capacities (Ashenafi 2003; Mondlane 2003; An-Na'im 2003; Gahamanyi 2003). I employ five measures that capture the state capacity–capturing economic development and I include *per capita GDP* (constant 2000 $ from the World Bank data). I also include a measure of the *geographical size of the state*, which captures the physical area a state needs capacity to cover. Finally, I include two population measures—*population size* and *population growth*, which capture the level of population pressures.

Substantive Findings and Analysis

My analysis on NAS law and women's rights attainment is significant because once again a more nuanced understanding emerges when testing normative debates of NAS law with empirical analysis. The first substantive finding is NAS law reduces women's political attainment, supporting the critical perspective. However, when interacting NAS law and democracy, a more nuanced picture emerges which demonstrates that colonial legacy was the major driver in women's political disenfranchisement. As argued by Fallon (2008), NAS law institutions and community groups actually helped women remain organized until political opportunity structures came with democratic openings in the early 1990s. Therefore, when interacting NAS law and democracy I find that the interaction actually increases women's political attainment. The finding is substantive because it demonstrates that the problem of gender equity requires reform across all legal systems whether civil, common or NAS law. The other substantive finding in my study is that gender quotas are important in improving women's political rights attainment. Gender quotas usually allot a percentage of seats in parliament to women, therefore guaranteeing an increase in women lawmakers. Together my analyses suggest a more nuanced understanding when examining NAS law's relation to women's attainment.

EMPIRICAL FINDINGS AND ANALYSIS

I first estimate six OLS models and then estimate parallel fixed effects (FE) models to impose time independent effects for each entity in order to control for heterogeneity. Since I am running OLS regressions, the reported coefficient from the independent variables shows the size of effect and direction of effect, except on the logged variables. The coefficients are interpreted as a one-unit or percent change in X causes Y to increase or decrease by the reported coefficient. Table 4.2 reports the results. My analysis suggests a more nuanced understanding on NAS law's effect on women's rights attainment than either perspective recognizes. First, we can see the relation between NAS law and women's political attainment is negative. Despite arguments that NAS law institutions provide political opportunities for women within NAS law institutions, I find that NAS law in itself does not open access to

Table 4.2. Testing Protection to Political Attainment

	World Bank (1997–2013)	
Variable	*RE*	*FE*
Protection	0.01	0.01
	(0.02)	(0.02)
Level Democracy	0.01	0.01
	(0.01)	(0.01)
Interaction (Pro|Dem)	0.01	0.01
	(0.01)	(0.01)
CEDAW	**0.22**	**0.20**
	(0.04)	(0.04)
ICESCR	**–0.13**	**–0.15**
	(0.03)	(0.03)
CEDAW Opt	**0.05**	0.01
	(0.02)	(0.02)
ICESCR Opt	0.01	–0.05
	(0.07)	(0.07)
Reserved Seats Quota	**0.17**	0.09
	(0.05)	(0.05)
Candidate List Quota	**0.48**	**0.39**
	(0.08)	(0.08)
Party Volunteer Quota	0.03	0.05
	(0.06)	(0.06)
Log GDP per capita	–0.01	**–0.05**
	(0.02)	(0.02)
Log Geographical Size	**–0.04**	**–0.04**
	(0.01)	(0.01)
Log Population Total	**0.04**	0.03
	(0.02)	(0.02)
Population Growth	–0.01	–0.01
	(0.02)	(0.02)
Constant	**1.32**	**1.89**
	(0.33)	(0.33)
Observation	576	576
R-Sq	0.18	0.15

women in the state system. In fact, an increase in the level of legal provision for NAS law in state constitutions reduces the level of political attainment for women, supporting the critical argument. Furthermore, surprisingly, democracy in itself also does not appear to improve women's attainment. However, interestingly, I find that the interaction between NAS law and democracy appears to provide support for Fallon's (2008) argument. Fallon asserts that the rapid increase in women's political attainment in sub-Saharan Africa occurs because women were experienced and organized in the NAS law system and democratic political opportunity structures. These findings provide support in part for both schools of thought. The colonial governments' support for male attainment appears to have marginalized women's attainment relative to men at all levels of society whether in the civil, common, or NAS law systems, thus reform of all legal systems is necessary. Second, some support suggests that women's organizations and political experiences in NAS law systems helped women to take advantage of the new structural opportunities that came about during the democratization period.

When examining the standard-based rights World Bank model, protection of NAS law had no effect on women's political attainment. Next, I address the other variables in the models. First, I examine international treaties; I find that international rights treaties have a mixed effect. A one-unit increase in CEDAW increases the percentage of women in parliament in all models by approximately 0.20 percent. Furthermore, a one-unit increase in the ICESCR decreases women's political attainment by about –0.13 percent in the World Bank model. Turning to the quota types in Table 4.2, quotas appear to help in improving women's rights attainment as expected.[9] As argued by Paxton and others (2010), quotas turn out to be an important factor that improves women's political attainment. [10] A one-unit increase in reserved seats quotas increases women's political attainment in the World Bank random effects models by approximately 0.17. When analyzing the candidate list quotas, women's political attainment improves across all models by approximately 0.45 percent. In addition, as expected, a 1 percent increase in logged geographical size of the state decreases women's political attainment in the World Bank models by approximately 0.04 percent.

Together my analysis suggests a more nuanced understanding when examining NAS law's relation to women's attainment. While NAS law and democracy do not improve women's political attainment, their interaction appears to offer the political opportunities that enable women to take advantage of new democratic structures, complemented by political experience and organization under NAS law systems.

EXPERIMENTING WITH A TRICHOTOMOUS DEMOCRACY MEASURE

To further check my results, I ran 6 more models described in Table 4.3 using Davenport and Armstrong's (2004) categorization of the Polity IV 11-point scale into a trichotomous measure with "1" depicting low levels of democracy (0-7), "2" depicting a medium level of democracy (8-9) and "3" depicting high levels of democracy (10). I note that the Davenport and Armstrong

Table 4.3. Trichotomous Democracy Measure

	World Bank (1997–2013)	
Variable	*RE*	*FE*
Protection	**–2.34**	**–2.66**
	(0.54)	(0.55)
Level Democracy	**–3.22**	**–3.51**
	(0.71)	(0.72)
Interaction (Pro|Dem)	**0.90**	**1.08**
	(0.34)	(0.34)
CEDAW	1.36	1.06
	(0.80)	(0.80)
ICESCR	**–3.12**	**–3.23**
	(0.59)	(0.60)
CEDAW Opt	**1.39**	0.63
	(0.40)	(0.43)
ICESCR Opt	**–3.81**	**–4.90**
	(1.12)	(1.19)
Reserved Seats Quota	**6.81**	**5.39**
	(0.97)	(1.02)
Candidate List Quota	**16.33**	**15.03**
	(1.33)	(1.39)
Party Volunteer Quota	**2.89**	**2.99**
	(1.08)	(1.07)
Log GDP per capita	**2.45**	**1.85**
	(0.34)	(0.37)
Log Geographical Size	**–2.28**	**–2.28**
	(0.28)	(0.28)
Log Population Total	**3.32**	**3.12**
	(0.38)	(0.38)
Population Growth	–0.19	–0.16
	(0.36)	(0.36)
Constant	**–35.60**	**–26.53**
	(6.26)	(6.59)
Observation	707	707
R-sq	0.36	0.35

(2004) measure has been recently challenged by Richards, Webb, and Clay (2015), who challenge that the authors cut points on democracy; however, I assert the measure still provides a good estimate in checking my results. The trichotomous models further confirmed my analysis that NAS law interaction with democracy increases the level of political rights attainment. Across all the models the interaction between democracy and NAS law increases women's political attainment. In addition, the trichotomies measure also confirms that the protection of NAS law in state constitutions consistently reduces the level of political attainment across all levels. When I examine all other variables, the trichotomous variable produces even stronger support across all categories for the previous model. The major changes appear to be on GDP per capita, and the effect of GDP per capita appears to be particularly important as it increases women's attainment consistently across all models, showing that a state's economic capacity plays an important role in improving women's attainment.

CONCLUSION

Critics of NAS law have often argued that it bears responsibility for the gender gap, while the positive perspective proponents have argued that NAS law is a viable system that can enhance women's attainment. The statistical analysis provides strong evidence that NAS law's effect on women's rights attainment requires more empirical analysis. My analysis demonstrates that NAS law impedes women's political attainment, and at the same time, my analysis also provides evidence that NAS law interaction with democracy does improve women's attainment. These findings have a number of interesting implications for the broader NAS law literature and human rights studies. My analysis sheds light on the relation between NAS law legal provisions' effect on women's attainment, which is important because NAS law has strong influence on matters that deal with family law and property law that directly affects the majority of the people in sub-Saharan Africa. My findings suggest that more studies should be done on how NAS law plays a role in women's organization and community groups, and why NAS law appears to reduce women's ability to progress in state government. My study also offers a more in-depth examination beyond the general assumptive conclusion that NAS law is negative. I argue that continuous evolution of NAS law is essential, as would be appropriate with any other type of law. While there are areas in which NAS law may require revisions, it may be erroneous and misguided to assume that all principles of NAS law reduce women's attainment. I find that when interacting with democracy, NAS law does improve women's political attainment. In part, this brings support to Fallon's argument that within NAS law institutions, women had political opportunities and organization; however, they remained marginalized from the state system until the onset of democratization in the 1990s. This insight can be useful in doing further examinations on what elements of democracy open opportunity structures for women to participate in state politics, and whether NAS law has a part to play in women's political empowerment. Furthermore, an interesting potential link may be between the existence of quotas for political participation and NAS. Examining the interaction between quotas for political participation and NAS law may explain the rapid increase in women's representation in sub-Saharan Africa.

NOTES

1. As explained in chapter 2, I redefine and conceptualize customary law as neo-autogenous law (NAS law) because a majority of the law emerged from the indigenous sub-Saharan population and was revived or modified by external influences (mostly from colonial experience).

2. UNDP, Millennium Development Goals: Promote gender equality and empower women–where do we stand?, http://www.undp.org/content/undp/en/home/mdgoverview/mdg_goals/mdg3/.

3. Fallon, Kathleen M., *Democracy and the Rise of Women's Movements in Sub-Saharan Africa*, (Baltimore: Johns Hopkins University Press, 2008), pp 4.

4. Ibid.

5. Ibid.

6. UN Women, Facts and Figures: Leadership and Political Participation-Women in parliaments, http://www.unwomen.org/en/what-we-do/leadership-and-political-participation/facts-and-figures#sthash.BiVPTrsk.dpuf.

7. Inter-Parliamentary Union, Women in National Parliaments, http://www.ipu.org/wmn-e/classif.htm.

8. The Gender Quota Project, http://www.quotaproject.org/uid/search.cfm.

9. I ran preliminary models with quota sources and they had no impact except two unrelated findings.

10. From preliminary models, I found that NAS law does not affect quotas. Further, I did preliminary interactions with protection and quotas and found that protection has harmful effects both in the presence of quotas and without them.

Chapter Five

Implications and Conclusions

The contributions of this book welcome much discourse and debate because instead of asserting the popular notion that NAS law is a negative part of sub-Saharan Africa, most of my findings demonstrated a more nuanced understanding and complexity on the subject of NAS law. I find that while there are areas in which NAS law may require revisions, it may also be erroneous and misguided to assume that all principles of NAS law are negative. Theoretically, the idea that the global set of states are moving toward liberal norm constitutions does not ring true when examining constitutional provisions protecting NAS law. Constitutional complexification is occurring with synthesizing prior legal elements with global expected norms. In the sub-Saharan context, complexification plays out in the revision and adoption of NAS law as a part of the modern state under plural systems of law. Simply put, constitutions do matter, and as the descriptive data demonstrated, NAS law provisions have become central to the constitutional process. Therefore, it is important and necessary to continue the study of the legal type that is practiced across the entire continent. The continuous employment of NAS law in sub-Saharan Africa makes the topic important and demonstrates that it merits continuous examination by scholars and practitioners as demonstrated by the study.

Furthermore, when assessing how NAS law affects different issue areas, the book makes a major contribution as it pertains to property and women's rights. I present a more nuanced understanding that may, in part, deviate from the global expected norms. I argue that no perspective wholly dominates the debate by finding significant support that when applied correctly NAS law may improve land tenure and rights attainment. Such conclusions are substantive for policy makers when dealing with major issue areas in order to create effective policies. The misguided assumptions of what NAS law is and how it affects different aspects of the modern state has at times actually brought more harm than good. My work demonstrates the need to test empirically unquestioned and untested debates concerning NAS law. Modifications made to NAS law should respect sub-Saharan cultural rights while aiming to foster equity. NAS law continues to be a relevant form of social and political regulation that enjoys constitutional protection.

My book brings in other substantive contributions in the understanding of this legal type. I aimed to improve on the conceptualization of NAS law in order to help policy makers, legal scholars and political and policy scientists gain a new view of NAS law. I added to the discourse on the study redefining and conceptualizing customary law as "neo-autogenous sub-Saharan African law" or NAS law—autogenous means "emerging out of" and the qualifier, "neo" denoting "revived" or "modified." The conceptualization of NAS law provides a better understanding of the law's origins, a stronger foundation for a definitional framework, and acknowledges NAS law as a discrete form of law. Furthermore, I created and introduced an original, quantitative data set on customary law for all sub-Saharan states for the years 1952 to 2013, consisting of 196 state constitutions. In turn, I found significant levels of NAS law provisions in state constitutions, and that colonial legacy plays a major role in the protection of NAS law in state constitutions.

In the empirical chapters, I focused on the effect of NAS law on two important policy and academic areas: property transaction costs and women's political attainment. On property transaction costs, my analysis challenged the assumption that one of the two debates, the individualist or communalist perspective, has exclusive accuracy. I conclude that the communalist arguments have a high level of empirical support. For policy makers, my study suggested caution on the push toward one state-led statutory tenure law system, but should provide for property under tenure, while making succession laws more equitable. Turning to women's rights attainment, my research also provided a more nuanced understanding of NAS law's effect on women's rights and attainment. My analysis demonstrates that NAS law requires modification when it comes to women's access to political office. However, when controlling for the intersection between democracy and NAS law, I found that colonial political structures that gave way to the current political systems were male-centric and did not provide enfranchisement to women. Therefore, the problem may actually be in modifying not only NAS law, but also the modern state system to be more equitable.

The contributions of this book should make scholars and policy makers cautious when making arguments for and against the use of NAS law. Overall, I assert that there is need to engage in more empirical work when dealing with the subject of NAS law to test debates that surround the study. My book demonstrates that law remains a pivotal and essential part of the sub-Saharan sociopolitical and legal formation. My research shows that the erroneous and misguided assumption that NAS law refers to merely daily customs unworthy of academic consideration leads to legal studies overlooking the significance of the unique but widely practiced legal formation known as NAS law. Overall, I strongly suggest that the subject of sub-Saharan NAS law merits further and continuous consideration by scholars.

My findings set a definitional framework for NAS law and empirically examines provisions in state constitutions. There is also a clear narrative in the study that NAS law should evolve as a discrete law offering greater protection to all members in order to deal with the many changes in current Africa. The Bhe and Shibi cases demonstrate the need to understand the core principles of the law and not just the application. Lawmakers should use NAS law principles to improve on the protection afforded to groups living under the legal type. The various revisions, like the codification of NAS law, will ensure the continuous revision of NAS law in an equitable manner that respects sub-Saharan cultural rights. I argue that continuous evolution of NAS law is essential, as would be appropriate with any other type of law.

I believe my study can be of great value to several subject areas including human rights, family law, social structures, political science, and conflict studies. Future studies can add to this work by capturing NAS law processes on the ground across sub-Saharan Africa, providing a richer analysis on the effects of the law. Future researchers can also build on my work by examining the status of NAS law in comparison to statutory law and other state laws. Researchers can also examine the domestic constitutional bargaining process that shapes the constitution promulgation process to explain why NAS law provision continues to be part of the legal landscape.

Bibliography

Allott, A. N., "What Is to Be Done with African Customary Law? The Experience of Problems and Reforms in Anglophone Africa from 1950," *Journal of African Law* 28 (1984) ½.

An-Na'im, Abdullahi Ahmed, *Human Rights Under African Constitutions*, (Philadelphia: University of Pennsylvania Press, 2003).

An-Na'im, Abdullahi Ahmed. "State Responsibility Under International Human Rights Law to Change Religious and Customary Law." *Human Rights of Women: National and International Perspectives*, edited by Rebecca J. Cook, pages, (Philadelphia: University of Pennsylvania Press, 1994).

Anderson, Terry Lee, ed. *Property Rights and Indian Economies*. Rowman & Littlefield, 1992.

Anderson, Terry Lee, Bruce Lowell Benson, and Thomas E. Flanagan, eds. *Self-determination: The Other Path for Native Americans*. (Palo Alto: Stanford University Press, 2006).

Apodaca, Clair, "Women's Economic and Social Rights Achievement," *Human Rights Quarterly* 20 (Feb.,1998) 1 pp/ 139–172.

Ault, E. David & Gilbert L.Rutman, "The Development of Individual Rights to Property in Tribal Africa," *Journal of Law and Economics*, 22(1979)1: 163–182.

Avdeyna, O. (2007). "When Do States Comply with International Treaties? Policies on Violence against Women in Post-Communist Countries," *International Studies Quarterly* 51: 877–900.

Barnett, Donald & Karari Njama, *Mau Mau from Within* (New York & London: Monthly Review Press, 1966).

Barker, Joanne. *Native Acts: Law, Recognition, and Cultural Authenticity*. (Durham: Duke University Press, 2011).

Barrows, Richard & Micheal Roth, "Land Tenure and Investment in African Agriculture: Theory and Evidence," *The Journal of Mordern African Studies*, 28 (1990) 2: 265–297.

Bennett, T W, *Customary Law in Theory*, (Cape Town: Juta & Co, Ltd, 1991).

Bohannan, Paul, and Laura Bohannan, *Tiv Economy* (Evanston: Northwestern University Press, 1968).

Boli-Bennett, John, *The expansion of nation-states, 1870–1970*, (Ph.D. diss, Stanford University–Department of Sociology, 1976).

Charlesworth, Hilary. "What Are Women's International Human Rights"? *Human Rights of Women: National and International Perspectives*, edited by Rebecca J. Cook, pages, (Philadelphia: University of Pennsylvania Press, 1994).

Chanock, Martin, "A Peculiar Sharpness: An Essay on Property in the History of Customary Law in Colonial Africa," *The Journal of African History*, 32(1991) 1.

Chimhowu, Admos, and Phil Woodhouse. "Customary vs Private Property Rights? Dynamics and Trajectories of Vernacular Land Markets in Sub-Saharan Africa." *Journal of Agrarian Change 6*, no. 3 (2006): 346–371.

Cook, Rebecca J. "Women's International Human Rights Law: The Way Forward." *Human Rights of Women: National and International Perspectives*, edited by Rebecca J. Cook, pages, (Philadelphia: University of Pennsylvania Press, 1994).

Cole, David, "Idea of Humanity: Human Rights and Immigrants' Rights," *Human Rights Law Review*, 37 (2005).

Cornel University Law School, 18 U.S.C. § 1151–Indian Country Defined, http://www.law.cornell.edu/uscode/text/18/1151.

Crowder, Michael. "Indirect rule—French and British style." *Africa* 34 (1964) 03.

Cuskelly, Katrina, *Customs and Constitutions: State Recognition of Customary Law Around the World*, (Bangkok: IUCN, 2011).

Dahl, Robert Alan, *Democracy and Its Critics*, (New Haven: Yale University Press, 1989).

Department of Justice, Country Policy and Information Note, Kenya: Female Genital Mutilation (FGM), July 2017, https://www.justice.gov/eoir/page/file/982121/download.

De Soto, Hernando, *The Other Path: The Informal Revolution*, (New York: Basic Books, 1989).

De Soto, Hernando, *The Mystery of Capital: Why Capitalism Succeeds in the West and Fails Everywhere Else*, (New York: Basic Books, 2000).

Donnelly, Jack, *International Human Rights*, (Boulder: Westview Press, 2013).

Dussias, Allison M. "Squaw Drudges, Farm Wives, and the Dann Sisters' Last Stand: American Indian Women's Resistance to Domestication and the Denial of Their Property Rights." *NCL Rev*. 77 (1998): 637.

Englehart, Neil A. and Melissa K. Miller, "The CEDAW Effects: International Law's Impact on Women's Rights" *Journal of Human Rights* 13 (2014) 1.

Fallon, Kathleen M. *Democracy and the Rise of Women's Movements in Sub-Saharan Africa*. (Baltimore: Johns Hopkins University Press, 2008).

Frymer, Paul, "Law and American Political Development," *Law & Social Inquiry*, 33 (2008) 3.

Frymer, Paul, "Acting When Elected Officials Won't: Federal Courts and Civil Rights Enforcement in U.S. Labor Unions, 1935–85," *The American Political Science Review* 97 (2003) 3.

Galanter, Marc, "Why the 'Haves' Come out Ahead: Speculations on the Limits of Legal Change," *Law & Society Review* 9 (1974) 1.

Go, Julian, "A Globalizing Constitutionalism? Views from the Postcolony, 1945-2000," *International Sociology* 18 (2003) 1.

Goodliffe, J., and D.G. Hawkins. (2006). 'Explaining Commitment: States and the Convention Against Torture,' *The Journal of Politics*, 68 (2): 358–71.

GPO, 25 U.S.C. 2205 - Tribal probate codes; acquisitions of fractional interests by tribes, http://www.gpo.gov/fdsys/granule/USCODE-2010-title25/USCODE-2010-title25-chap24-sec2205/content-detail.html.

Grant, Evadne, "Human Rights, Cultural Diversity and Customary Law in South Africa," *Journal of African Law*, 50 (2006) 1.

Hafner-Burton, E., and K.Tsutsui. (2005). 'Human Rights in a Globalizing World: The Paradox of Empty Promises,' *The American Journal of Sociology*, 110 (5): 1373–1411.

Haynie, Stacia C. Neal Tate, Reginald Sheehan, and Donald R. Songer. 2001. "Winners and Losers: A Comparative Analysis of Appellate Courts and Litigation Outcomes." Paper presented at the American Political Science Association.

Held, David, *Models of Democracy*, (Cambridge: Polity Press, 2006).

Hydén, Göran. *African Politics in Comparative Perspective*. (Cambridge: Cambridge University Press, 2006 and 2013).

Joireman, Sandra F. "Enforcing new property rights in Sub-Saharan Africa: The Ugandan constitution and the 1998 land act." *Comparative Politics* (2007): 463–480.

Joireman, S.F., "The Mystery of Capital Formation in Sub-Saharan Africa: Women, Property Rights and Customary Law," *World Development* 36 (2007) 7.

Kagwanja, Peter. "Blaming the Environment: Ethnic Violence and the Political Economy of Displacement in Kenya." Occasional Paper Series 1, 2(2002).

Karns, Margaret P. & Karen A. Mingst. *International Organizations: The Political and Process of Global Governance*, (Boulder: Lynee Reinner Publishers, 2010).

Keith, Linda Camp, Political Repression: *Courts and Law*, (Philadelphia: University of Pennsylvania Press, 2012).

Keith, L.C. (1999). 'The United Nations International Covenant on Civil and Political Rights: Does It Make a Difference in Human Rights Behavior?' *Journal of Peace Research*, 36 (1): 95–118.

Kenyatta, Jomo, *Facing Mount Kenya* (New York: Vintage Books, 1965).

Landman, T. (2005). *Protecting Human Rights: A Comparative Study*, Washington, D.C.: Georgetown University Press.

Leakey, L.S.B, *The Southern Kĩkũyũ before 1903*: Vol 1, 2, 3 (London: Academic Press, 1977).

Leblang, David A., "Property Rights, Democracy and Economic Growth," *Political Science Quarterly*, 49 5 (1996).

Lipjhart, Arend, *Patterns of Democracy*, (New Haven: Yale University Press, 1999).

Louis, Henry Gates Jr., *Africa's Great Civilizations*, PBS, Acc 2-16-18, http://www.pbs.org/show/africas-great-civilizations/.

McCulley, Kristina L. "The American Indian Probate Reform Act of 2004: The Death of Fractionation or Individual Native American Property Interests and Tribal Customs?" *American Indian Law Review* 30, no. 2 (2005): 401–422.

Meyer, John w., John Boli, George M. Thomas & Francisco O. Ramirez, "World Society and the Nation-State," *American Journal of Sociology* 103 (July, 1997) 1.

Mamdani, Mahmood, *Citizen and Subject: Contemporary Africa and the Legacy of Late Colonialism*, (Princeton: Princeton University Press, 1996).

Morris, Clarence ed., *The Great Legal Philosophers: Selected Readings in Jurisprudence*, (Philadelphia, University of Pennsylvania Press, 1971), Ch. 10.

Motley, Kimberley, *How I Defend the Rule of Law*, TEDGlobal 2014, https://www.ted.com/talks/kimberley_motley_how_i_defend_the_rule_of_law.

NARF, Native American Rights Fund: Current Cases & Projects–Individual Indian Money Accounts–Cobell v. Kempthorne, http://www.narf.org/cases/iim.html.

O'Grady, Siobhan, Most girls in Somalia experience genital mutilation. The ritual just killed a 10-year-old, Washington Post, July 20 2018, https://www.washingtonpost.com/news/worldviews/wp/2018/07/20/most-girls-in-somalia-experience-genital-mutilation-the-ritual-just-killed-a-10-year-old/?noredirect=on&utm_term=.3793721e7cd6.

Olson, Susan M., "Interest-Group Litigation in Federal District Court: Beyond the Political Disadvantage Theory," *The Journal of Politics* 52 (1990) 3.

OYEZ, The Oyez Project at Chicago-Kent: Cases, http://www.oyez.org/.

Poe, Steven C., Dierdre Wendel-Blunt and Karl Ho, "Global Patterns in the Achievement of Women's Human Rights to Equality," *Human Rights Quarterly* 19 (Nov., 1997) 4 pp.813-835.

Paxton, Pamela, Melanie M. Hughes, Matthew A. Painter II, "Growth in Women's Political Representation: A Longitudinal Exploration of Democracy, Electoral System and Gender Quotas," *European Journal of Political Research*, 49 (2010)

Reid, Kathryn, World Vision, FGM: Kenyan girls, boys 'throw away' culture that causes pain, Feb 1, 2018, https://www.worldvision.org/gender-equality-news-stories/female-genital-mutilation-fgm.

Reynold, Andrew, *Designing Democracy in a Dangerous World*, (Oxford, Oxford University Press, 2011).

Richards and Haglund, *Violence Against Women and the Law*, (New York: Routledge book, 2015).

Riley, Angela R. "Tribal Sovereignty in a Post-9/11 World." *NDL Rev*. 82 (2006): 953.

Sheleff, Leon. *The Future of Tradition: Customary Law, Common Law and Legal Pluralism*. (London: Frank Cass, 2000).

Simmance, A. J. F., "Land Redemption Among the Fort Hall Kikuyu," *Journal of African Law* 5 (1961) 2.

Simmons, Beth A., "International Law and State Behavior: Commitment and Compliance in International Monetary," *The American Political Science Review* 94 (Dec., 20000 4 pp. 819–835

Simmons, Beth A., *Mobilizing for Human Rights: International Law in Domestic Politics*. (Cambridge: Cambridge University Press, 2009).

Stewart, William H., *Concepts of Federalism*, (Lanham, University Press of America, 1984), 80–82.

Tripp, Aili Mari, "Women's Movements, Customary Law and Land Rights in Africa: The Case of Uganda," *African Studies Quarterly*, 7 (2004) 4.

UN Women, End Violence Against Women Now, http://www.endvawnow.org/en/articles/625-polygamous-marriages.html.

University of Ottowa Juriglobe Project, Country geographic size in thousands (size-thou)–Juriglobe: http://www.juriglobe.ca/eng/index.php.

Watts, Ronald, *Comparing Federal Systems in the 1990s* (Kingston: Queens University, 1996).

World Bank, Doing Business Data, http://www.doingbusiness.org/methodology.

Wotipka & Ramirez 2003–Wotipka, C.M., and F.O. Ramirez. (2007). 'World Society and Human Rights: An Event History Analysis of the Convention on the Elimination of All Forms of Discrimination against Women,' in B.A. Simmons, G. Garrett, and F. Dobbin (eds.), *The Global Diffusion of Markets and Democracy*, Cambridge: Cambridge University Press.

Zakaria, Fareed, *The Future of Freedom: Illiberal Democracy at Home and Abroad*, (New York: WW Norton and Company, 2007).

Index

Page references for figures are italicized

About the Author

Dr. Casper Njuguna is an African politics, international relations and law scholar and expert. He received his doctorate from the University of Texas at Dallas in Political Science. Dr. Njuguna has vast experience having worked in non-governmental, governmental and academic institutions. He was formerly a director and senior policy advisor at Africa Policy Institute. He has served as a lecturer and professor at various universities. His research interests focus on comparative studies examining institutions and process in sub-Saharan Africa and America. Dr. Njuguna also serves as young adult minister and his relationship with the LORD Jesus defines his world view.

www.ingramcontent.com/pod-product-compliance
Ingram Content Group UK Ltd.
Pitfield, Milton Keynes, MK11 3LW, UK
UKHW041122071026
15587UKWH00009B/69

9 781498 584401